AMERICAN HERITAGE
ILLUSTRATED HISTORY
OF THE UNITED STATES

Banastre Tarleton's cavalry in a skirmish in January, 1781.

AMERICAN HERITAGE ILLUSTRATED HISTORY OF THE UNITED STATES

VOLUME 3

THE REVOLUTION

BY ROBERT G. ATHEARN

Created in Association with the
Editors of AMERICAN HERITAGE

and for the updated edition
MEDIA PROJECTS INCORPORATED

CHOICE PUBLISHING, INC.
New York

Library of Congress Catalog Card Number: 87-73399
ISBN 0-945260-03-2
ISBN 0-945260-00-8

This 1988 edition is published and distributed by Choice Publishing, Inc., 53 Watermill Lane, Great Neck, NY 11021 by arrangement with American Heritage, a division of Forbes, Inc.

Manufactured in the United States of America
10 9 8 7 6 5 4 3

CONTENTS OF THE COMPLETE SERIES

Editor's Note to the Revised Edition
Introduction by ALLAN NEVINS
Main text by ROBERT G. ATHEARN

EACH VOLUME CONTAINS AN ENCYCLOPEDIC SECTION; MASTER INDEX IN VOLUME 18

CONTENTS OF VOLUME 3

CHAPTER 7

RABBLE IN ARMS

The Continental Association, framed at the meeting of the First Continental Congress in the fall of 1774, was no mere oratorical expression of resistance against England. It was the beginning of a struggle for independence. From New Hampshire to South Carolina, the colonies united in agreeing on a group of pledges to protect their rights.

If those on this side of the Atlantic recognized the seriousness of the situation, George III did not. Stubbornly he told his prime minister, Lord North, that a state of rebellion existed, and that, while Britain yielded not an inch, "blows must decide whether they are to be subject to this country or independent." To his surprise, the colonials met his challenge.

During the winter of 1774–75, antagonism between British troops and the colonials heightened. While General Thomas Gage concentrated his troops around Boston, neighboring villagers, angered by the threat of military action, quietly gathered pow-

American patriots, full of the feeling of their independence, pull down the statue of George III in New York in July, 1776.

der and ball. Gage learned from his spies that in the village of Concord, 21 miles from Boston, there was a major supply depot, and that in Lexington, five miles from Concord, there were a couple of incendiaries named Samuel Adams and John Hancock.

After some temporizing, Gage dispatched 700 soldiers to capture the two men and destroy the supplies. As Gage's men marched on the evening of April 18, Paul Revere, William Dawes, and Dr. Samuel Prescott sped on horseback through the night to warn of the redcoats' advance. The colonials turned out, and when Gage's troops appeared at Lexington at dawn, they were met by 38 villagers in military formation. In the ensuing exchange of shots, eight Americans died and nine were wounded. Leaving the rebels to count their losses, His Majesty's troops now moved on to Concord. The first blood in the American Revolution had been drawn.

After the supplies in Concord were destroyed, Gage's troops fought off an attack at the Old North Bridge, suffering 14 casualties, and began the return march. Angry farmers all over the area snatched rifles from

COLLECTION OF COLONEL R. V. C. BODLEY

General Thomas Gage was commander of the British forces in America, 1763–1775.

above their fireplaces and swarmed after the red line. Under fire, the British troops stumbled along, men falling dead with frightening regularity. When 1,200 reinforcements with two fieldpieces arrived, the fighting sharpened. By night, the British were safe in Charlestown, but the journey to Concord had cost them 247 in killed and wounded. The American "rabble," who were not supposed to be a match for the king's men, had lost 88.

A time for decision

The encounter at Lexington and Concord was of no great military significance, yet it was a symbol to colonials. Lord North's government had already begun to relax certain restrictions, but fast-moving events nullified his conciliating efforts. The king, upon

hearing from General Gage, said firmly that "America must be a colony of England or treated as an enemy." Americans all along the Atlantic Coast were equally angered by the affair. In Virginia, George Washington announced that now it was either war or slavery. In South Carolina, two regiments of troops were easily formed. During these heated days, delegates to the Second Continental Congress were traveling toward Philadelphia, where they would meet on May 10, 1775.

The skirmish in the Massachusetts villages now became a flaming challenge, and because of it the delegates to the Second Continental Congress were faced with new and perplexing problems. They had talked merely of resistance the year before; now they were called upon to decide more dangerous questions. Their very existence was revolutionary. The home government had prohibited them even from meeting, and their assembling was in direct violation of the law. Resolved to proceed under any circumstances, they began their sessions. Soon it was apparent that delegates from all the colonies were in favor of supporting Massachusetts in her time of need. Although the delegates denied any plans for independence, they stood by the rights of the colonies to resist what they regarded as oppression.

When the Continental Army was formed, and Washington placed at its head, Congress justified the action by publishing a declaration setting forth "the Causes and Necessities of Taking Up Arms." Independence was not mentioned. But the document's words sounded ominously like it: "Our cause is just. Our union is perfect. Our internal resources are great. . . ." Despite the strength of the moderates in the gathering, the force of circumstance would propel Americans down the road to independence. Perhaps they did not know it, but they had passed the point of no return.

The Battle of Bunker Hill

Already fate was setting in place the combustibles of final separation. General Gage, now reinforced, resolved to strengthen his fortifications around Boston by occupying nearby heights. He began his movements in mid-June of 1775, and was at once answered by Massachusetts militiamen, who dug in atop Breed's Hill. British warships in the harbor lobbed shells at the militiamen while infantry units stormed their position. Twice the British were driven off, but on the third assault they routed the Americans, whose powder supply had been exhausted. Thus the battle, misnamed after adjacent Bunker Hill, ended. It was neither a great victory for the British nor a signal defeat for the Americans. But the fact of the battle was significant, for it indicated to the British that there was growing in America a determination to fight. Many along the Atlantic seaboard were thrilled by this example of American armed resistance to the overwhelming power of England.

The day before Bunker Hill, George

Paul Revere was painted at his silversmith's workbench by John Singleton Copley.

Washington accepted from the Continental Congress command of the Continental Army at Philadelphia; by early July he was at Cambridge ready for active duty. Here he found a mob of approximately 16,000 men, mostly from Massachusetts. Soon Congress supplied him with 3,000 more from the middle colonies. All in all, it was a strange array. There were no uniforms; shades of brown and green stood out among multicolored clothing. Washington suggested that hunting shirts be worn "to unite the men and abolish those provincial distinctions." Officers were elected by their men, a custom to continue for some time in the American armed forces, and rather than demand the privileges of rank, many officers even did somewhat menial tasks to gain their men's favor. Among the

officers of highest rank, commissioned by Congress, there were dissatisfactions; each felt he was entitled to a position of greater importance and responsibility. General Washington had little to make him optimistic as he set forth to bring order out of chaos.

The house divided

Events like Lexington and Concord, followed by the larger battle at Breed's Hill, cut sharply through the strata of American society. Many men who previously had accepted things as they were now had to declare themselves for or against independence. Conservatives and, in general, those who held offices in America struggled to maintain the connection with England. They angered those who regarded war as the only course, and with each violent incident the breach widened. Radical leaders like Sam Adams, who had urged independence for nearly a decade, seized upon the division and fanned the flames of revolution to white heat. Another firebrand, Thomas Paine, published his pamphlet *Common Sense,* and at once it became a best seller. The propagandist, as always, had put into words what many men had been thinking but could not say.

The British seemed continually to

With some of their men bareheaded and wounded, the British troops form into columns and to the sound of drums march stoically across the trampled grass and up Breed's Hill—in a painting by Howard Pyle.

provide reasons for colonial charges against them. The king had already announced that blows must decide the issue, and when he received what was called the Olive Branch Petition from the colonies, he rejected it, stigmatizing all Americans as disloyal. The moderate William Pitt proposed a compromise, but Parliament rejected it. In October, 1775, the Continental Congress learned that Falmouth, Maine, had been burned by a British naval force, and three months later Norfolk, Virginia, was razed. Each occurrence underscored the charges of men like Sam Adams and Tom Paine that King George was not infallible and that perhaps he was a "royal brute" after all. Inevitably the road led toward revolution.

The declaration

As early as April, 1776, Richard Henry Lee, head of a great Virginia family, advised Patrick Henry that immediate independence was a necessity because the home government had placed the colonies in a position of anarchy. Here was a man whose sons were then at school in England, whose brother was an official in London, and whose own living came from the sale of tobacco in English markets. Yet he saw no alternative to taking the extreme step.

Not everyone agreed with him. But a month later, on May 15, Virginia passed resolutions, saying their delegates to Congress ought to propose independence. And on June 7, Lee of-fered a resolution that the colonies were free and independent states, having no further allegiance to Great Britain. But Congress, like most groups, had its conservatives, and they were opposed to declaring a state of independence. Edward Rutledge of South Carolina led the opposition, which argued that to take a position before doing anything to maintain it was foolish.

About all the conservatives could do was gain a delay of three weeks. During the last days of June, while the debate continued, Lee's fellow Virginian, Thomas Jefferson, along with Benjamin Franklin, John Adams, Roger Sherman, and Robert R. Livingston, worked out a draft of an independence declaration. And on July 2, Congress passed the Lee resolution that the American colonies were independent of England. John Adams predicted that the date would "be celebrated by succeeding generations as the great anniversary Festival." But it was not. July 4, when the amended and revised declaration was approved, was to become the anniversary date.

The Declaration of Independence was not intended to be in any sense radical. Jefferson himself said he did not attempt to incorporate anything new or startling, that he simply tried to present "an expression of the American mind." There were two main parts to the Declaration—a preamble and a catalogue of grievances. It was in the preamble that Jefferson and his associates turned to the writings of

John Locke, an English political philosopher, in search of a general justification for what they were about to do. They borrowed so heavily from Locke that they even used several of his phrases. The heart of their argument was that "all men are created equal, that they are endowed by their Creator with certain unalienable Rights; that among them are Life, Liberty, and the pursuit of Happiness." Thus paraphrasing a writer well known to Americans of their day, Jefferson and the others sketched out the right of revolution under certain conditions of oppression. It was their contention that if the British government was unwilling to grant a portion of its subjects the rights they considered basic, those so denied might, with justification, break away.

The second main part of the Decla-

The redcoats swarm over Breed's Hill in their third assault as the British Major John Pitcairn (right), mortally wounded, is carried from the field, and patriot Dr. Joseph Warren (left) dies. The painting is by John Trumbull.

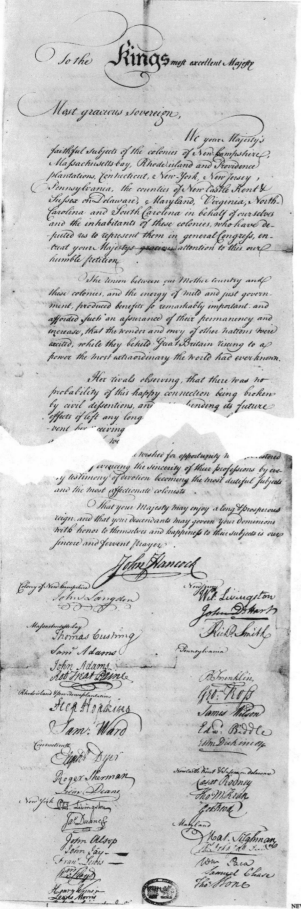

ration was a bill of particulars stating why the American move for independence was a necessity. The list was a long one, aimed at the king, who was accused of all manner of injustices to the colonials. It was meant to arouse Americans and bring sympathy from those in England who did not like George III. The indictment against him referred to the dissolution of colonial legislatures, the hindrance of immigration, the packing of government offices in America, the "illegal" quartering of troops in the colonies, and the imposition of taxes without the consent of those taxed. The authors of the Declaration concluded this portion of their indictment with the comment that George III was "unfit to be the ruler of a free People." The only reference to Parliament was the statement that the Americans had warned their British cousins "of attempts by their legislature to extend an unwarrantable jurisdiction over us." In conclusion, the signatories declared the independence of the American colonies from Great Britain and a total dissolution of any and all previous connections with the crown.

None of the charges got to the root of the matter. Perhaps not even Jefferson could have done so. The alienation had come about so gradually that few could isolate the real reasons for discontent. Jefferson would have had to describe the history of each of the col-

The Olive Branch Petition, as John Adams named it, was flatly rejected by George III.

onies from its original grant of political powers. He might have pointed out that conservatives tended to stay home and liberals tended to migrate, thus weighting the population in America with those inclined to independence. But such reasons were general and intangible. They would not have been convincing to those who were to take up the struggle and carry it on. This is perhaps why Jefferson dealt with specific and recent, if somewhat unsupportable, charges of mistreatment at the hands of the king.

Uniting the states

A few days after its approval by Congress, the Declaration was publicly read in Philadelphia, the seat of the newborn government. John Adams wrote that there was great and boisterous rejoicing. "The bells rang all day and almost all night." Before long it was read in other colonies, too, with the same reaction.

The writing and promulgation of the Declaration proved to be a master stroke on the part of those in Congress who had strongly supported independence. Now it was too late to turn back. A new nation had been born, and even those who had clung to the hope of remaining a part of the Empire were obliged to support it or suffer the consequences. That the sentiment was fixed in writing and that its supporters had signed it seemed to legalize it and make it permanent.

Although the Declaration provided the emergent nation with clear-cut

Patrick Henry

war aims from the outset, many showed little enthusiasm for violence. These conservatives, who mostly had been associated with the Tories, recoiled from such a radical step as civil war. To be sure, many of them resented England's regulatory legislation, but the home government indisputably represented law and order. Being property holders, they wanted England's protection for their holdings. More than once she had intervened to save aristocratic colonials from the demands of the common people. Judging the present situation, the conservatives concluded it was safer to put up with Parliament, with all its restrictions, than to consort with the democratic experimenters.

At the time of the Declaration of Independence, perhaps one-third of the colonial population could be counted as loyalist. The group included officeholders, members of the Anglican Church, and the military. Not only did they have a high regard for the authority of the crown, but they were unwilling to cut all ties with the past in favor of a new and untried venture. They had no assurance that the result would be no more than a break with England. Revolutions often get out of hand, and should social upheaval accompany political change, men of property and high position would be the losers. About 60,000 loyalists left the colonies, electing not to take their chances with more daring Americans. Other thousands, who did not want to leave, quietly turned over their property to friends or relatives who were regarded favorably by the revolutionaries and sat out the storm, saying nothing.

The "patriots," or what might be called the Popular Party, were a mixture of radicals and men who simply went along, often reluctantly. The fighting core of this body found its strength in the left wing of the Whig Party in America and represented a triumph of the liberals over the conservatives. Many a man like John Dickinson, who opposed the move for independence, fought alongside his fellow Americans when the time for shooting came. Dickinson, a well-known colonial leader, humbly joined the Continental Army as a private.

The Popular Party was also diverse in the origins of its members. There were small farmers, artisans, frontiersmen, free-trade merchants, and even well-to-do Southern planters. The planters contributed Thomas Jefferson, George Mason, and, for a while, Patrick Henry. Most of them had no intention of participating in a movement that might develop along democratic lines. They felt that property must be protected, the rights of gentlemen preserved, and class status recognized. "We are not contending that our rabble or all unqualified persons shall have the right of voting," said one Southerner. With this in mind, the landed gentry guided the Revolution as a movement against England and closed their ears to talk about dividing the spoils when the fighting was over. So well did they accomplish their purpose of focusing the struggle on grievances against the mother country that the "revolution from within" was not fully recognized until after 1782.

War propaganda

In exciting their fellow Americans against the British Empire, propagandists on this side of the Atlantic did a first-rate job. All the weaknesses and corruptions of the mother country were dragged out to make her appear decadent and cruel and to be sucking the life out of the colonies in order to save herself. Americans were warned repeatedly that if they remained in the Empire, they would "see their property used to glut the avarice of half a million swag-bellied pensioners" in England. America of 1775 was made to appear as the virtuous child, obliged to support a bankrupt and profligate parent. Alexander Hamilton estimated that it would take Britain 120 years to pay off her existing debt provided she did not go to war, and he was sure there would be no such reign of peace. It was his firm belief that England's next war would be her last.

In England, meanwhile, there was a tendency to discount both the intentions and capabilities of the Americans. Propagandists worked hard to present the colonials as shaggy squirrel hunters, totally undisciplined and even lacking in courage. As the hardcore revolutionaries were descendants of Englishmen who had left home to brave the trials of life in the wilds of America, questioning their courage seemed hardly supportable. That it was an error would be proved again and again during the war. Others who discounted the chances of American success pointed out that there was no unity among the colonials. Here they were on stronger ground. Differences between the North and the South already were apparent, and those who doubted that they could be reconciled even in war were not far from right. The differences would be one of the major problems facing the leaders.

Propagandists on both sides were playing to an audience larger than at home. Anxious eyes were cast toward the Continent, for there lay the balance of power. Englishmen wanted no interference in what they regarded as a domestic disturbance, while Americans openly solicited foreign aid. France and Spain were the most likely to interfere. France still felt the pain of having nearly all her American co-

The Maryland Regiment leaves Annapolis on July 10, 1776, to join Washington.

lonial holdings taken by the British in 1763. Ever since, she had competed fiercely with the British, particularly in the Caribbean sugar islands, and her interest in transatlantic holdings had not died. Concurrently, Spain and England were at swords' points over commercial rivalries and had come nearly to blows in 1770. Both France and Spain yearned for a chance to strike at the proud mistress of the seas. They realized she got part of her strength from the thriving commerce of her American colonies, and in the hope of cutting it off, they listened to all the revolutionaries had to say.

Strategy of war

Regardless of propaganda, there *were* some long-range considerations. The British were faced by difficulties greater than they would admit. The land where they proposed to fight was over 3,000 miles away, and their opponent was skilled in warfare. Moreover, sympathy for America was so great in England that Hessian troops had to be hired to fight the colonials.

Although 15,000 or more troops were usually available in Great Britain, there were fewer than 5,000 in the fall of 1775. A large part of the British army was in America or the West Indies. The most effective force was the 9,000 men in Boston, but for the moment General Washington had them cornered. Americans controlled the Atlantic coastline. And capture of the major seaports would not quell the rebellion. The British would have to work inland, foot by foot, and subdue the rebels as they found them. But supply lines would grow aggravatingly long and expensive to maintain and casualties would mount alarmingly with each mile of advance.

On the other hand, if the Americans were as united as the Declaration of Independence suggested, they should have won their war in much less time. Despite such announcements of union, American individualism was never more than briefly submerged, and it would bob to the surface in quarrels among states, jealousies between sections, and in man-to-man bickering. Few wanted to serve in the Continental Army, and those who did often gave but a few months of their time. In America of 1776 there was a natural hostility to a large regular army. The struggle became a militiaman's war, with small groups turning out to fight under the leadership of some local officer like Francis Marion. Then, when the area was freed from immediate danger of invasion, the men went back to planting corn and haying. While they were willing to fight for their own communities, most colonials showed little interest in defending others. Thus, although several hundred thousand men may have participated in the war, few took part continuously or for long periods. Washington's army, at its peak of 18,000 in early 1776, fell to fewer than 5,000 before the war was over. It was enough to discourage the most hopeful of leaders.

THE
DECLARATION
OF
INDEPENDENCE

The famous event that Americans celebrate every Fourth of July was the formal beginning of the American Revolution. But the Declaration of Independence was more than a declaration of war. It was the first great document in the history of a nation whose name would come to be a symbol of freedom to all the world. The men who adopted it did not feel it to be anything new or radical in principle, for it expressed ideas that had become common property to leading minds of the 18th century. Yet it *was* new in announcing those ideas as the basis of an actual society. Its foundation was the theory of natural rights—ones to which all men were entitled simply by reason of being human, and which could not justly be taken from them: "Life, Liberty, and the pursuit of Happiness." From this followed logically the function of government, which was to make those rights more secure to every individual, by means of laws having the consent of the governed. But the Declaration marked the point of no return for the Revolution; it was not just a chapter in the history of ideas. The picture portfolio that follows illustrates some of the persons, places, and things associated with the dawning of the democratic epoch in the climactic summer of 1776.

	The Draw Bridge	To
	Buck Building	Ca
	Edw Shipn	Gr
	Ant Morris Brew House	Ins
	Capts Vine	W
	Jonathan Dickinson	Th

CRADLE OF REVOLUTION

Colonial Philadelphia is seen from the Delaware River in the pre-Revolution painting above. The many ships and substantial houses attest to the young city's metropolitan status. It was the most enterprising commercial center of America.

The building in Philadelphia where the Declaration was adopted and signed looked as it is at the left when the Continental Congress met there in 1776. Known as the State House, it was not called Independence Hall for another 75 years.

Nothing did more to rally public opinion to the cause of independence than Tom Paine's pamphlet *Common Sense,* of which the title page is shown at the right. His fiery eloquence convinced thousands that, as he put it, " 'Tis time to part!"

OVERLEAF: A detail from John Trumbull's celebrated painting, showing John Adams, Roger Sherman, Robert Livingston, Thomas Jefferson, and Benjamin Franklin, all members of the drafting committee, as they present the Declaration to Congress.

YALE UNIVERSITY ART GALLERY

COMMON SENSE;

ADDRESSED TO THE

INHABITANTS

O F

A M E R I C A,

On the following interesting

S U B J E C T S.

I. Of the Origin and Design of Government in general, with concise Remarks on the English Constitution.

II. Of Monarchy and Hereditary Succession.

III. Thoughts on the present State of American Affairs.

IV. Of the present Ability of America, with some miscellaneous Reflections.

Man knows no Master save creating HEAVEN,
Or those whom choice and common good ordain.
THOMSON.

PHILADELPHIA;
Printed, and Sold, by R. BELL, in Third-Street.
MDCCLXXVI.

THE SPIRIT OF '76

For the Centennial of the Declaration (right), Archibald M. Willard painted
the scene that has come to symbolize the spirit of the Revolution. The dis-
heartened Americans face defeat—until an indomitable trio of musicians ral-
lies them to fight anew for the independence the Declaration has proclaimed.

In CONGRESS, July 4, 1776.

The unanimous Declaration of the thirteen united States of America.

When in the Course of human events, it becomes necessary for one people to dissolve the political bands which have connected them with another, and to assume among the powers of the earth, the separate and equal station to which the Laws of Nature and of Nature's God entitle them, a decent respect to the opinions of mankind requires that they should declare the causes which impel them to the separation.

We hold these truths to be self-evident, that all men are created equal, that they are endowed by their Creator with certain unalienable Rights, that among these are Life, Liberty and the pursuit of Happiness. — That to secure these rights, Governments are instituted among Men, deriving their just powers from the consent of the governed, — That whenever any Form of Government becomes destructive of these ends, it is the Right of the People to alter or to abolish it, and to institute new Government, laying its foundation on such principles and organizing its powers in such form, as to them shall seem most likely to effect their Safety and Happiness. Prudence, indeed, will dictate that Governments long established should not be changed for light and transient causes; and accordingly all experience hath shewn, that mankind are more disposed to suffer, while evils are sufferable, than to right themselves by abolishing the forms to which they are accustomed. But when a long train of abuses and usurpations, pursuing invariably the same Object evinces a design to reduce them under absolute Despotism, it is their right, it is their duty, to throw off such Government, and to provide new Guards for their future security. — Such has been the patient sufferance of these Colonies; and such is now the necessity which constrains them to alter their former Systems of Government. The history of the present King of Great Britain is a history of repeated injuries and usurpations, all having in direct object the establishment of an absolute Tyranny over these States. To prove this, let Facts be submitted to a candid world.

He has refused his Assent to Laws, the most wholesome and necessary for the public good.
He has forbidden his Governors to pass Laws of immediate and pressing importance, unless suspended in their operation till his Assent should be obtained; and when so suspended, he has utterly neglected to attend to them.
He has refused to pass other Laws for the accommodation of large districts of people, unless those people would relinquish the right of Representation in the Legislature, a right inestimable to them and formidable to tyrants only.
He has called together legislative bodies at places unusual, uncomfortable, and distant from the depository of their public Records, for the sole purpose of fatiguing them into compliance with his measures.
He has dissolved Representative Houses repeatedly, for opposing with manly firmness his invasions on the rights of the people.
He has refused for a long time, after such dissolutions, to cause others to be elected; whereby the Legislative powers, incapable of Annihilation, have returned to the People at large for their exercise; the State remaining in the mean time exposed to all the dangers of invasion from without, and convulsions within.
He has endeavoured to prevent the population of these States; for that purpose obstructing the Laws for Naturalization of Foreigners; refusing to pass others to encourage their migrations hither, and raising the conditions of new Appropriations of Lands.
He has obstructed the Administration of Justice, by refusing his Assent to Laws for establishing Judiciary powers.
He has made Judges dependent on his Will alone, for the tenure of their offices, and the amount and payment of their salaries.
He has erected a multitude of New Offices, and sent hither swarms of Officers to harrass our people, and eat out their substance.
He has kept among us, in times of peace, Standing Armies without the Consent of our legislatures.
He has affected to render the Military independent of and superior to the Civil power.
He has combined with others to subject us to a jurisdiction foreign to our constitution, and unacknowledged by our laws; giving his Assent to their Acts of pretended legislation:
For Quartering large bodies of armed troops among us: — For protecting them, by a mock Trial, from punishment for any Murders which they should commit on the Inhabitants of these States: — For cutting off our Trade with all parts of the world: — For imposing Taxes on us without our Consent: — For depriving us in many cases, of the benefits of Trial by Jury: — For transporting us beyond Seas to be tried for pretended offences: — For abolishing the free System of English Laws in a neighbouring Province, establishing therein an Arbitrary government, and enlarging its Boundaries so as to render it at once an example and fit instrument for introducing the same absolute rule into these Colonies: — For taking away our Charters, abolishing our most valuable Laws, and altering fundamentally the Forms of our Governments: — For suspending our own Legislatures, and declaring themselves invested with power to legislate for us in all cases whatsoever.
He has abdicated Government here, by declaring us out of his Protection and waging War against us.
He has plundered our seas, ravaged our Coasts, burnt our towns, and destroyed the lives of our people.
He is at this time transporting large Armies of foreign Mercenaries to compleat the works of death, desolation and tyranny, already begun with circumstances of Cruelty & perfidy scarcely paralleled in the most barbarous ages, and totally unworthy the Head of a civilized nation.
He has constrained our fellow Citizens taken Captive on the high Seas to bear Arms against their Country, to become the executioners of their friends and Brethren, or to fall themselves by their Hands.
He has excited domestic insurrections amongst us, and has endeavoured to bring on the inhabitants of our frontiers, the merciless Indian Savages, whose known rule of warfare, is an undistinguished destruction of all ages, sexes and conditions.

In every stage of these Oppressions We have Petitioned for Redress in the most humble terms: Our repeated Petitions have been answered only by repeated injury. A Prince whose character is thus marked by every act which may define a Tyrant, is unfit to be the ruler of a free people.

Nor have We been wanting in attentions to our British brethren. We have warned them from time to time of attempts by their legislature to extend an unwarrantable jurisdiction over us. We have reminded them of the circumstances of our emigration and settlement here. We have appealed to their native justice and magnanimity, and we have conjured them by the ties of our common kindred to disavow these usurpations, which, would inevitably interrupt our connections and correspondence. They too have been deaf to the voice of justice and of consanguinity. We must, therefore, acquiesce in the necessity, which denounces our Separation, and hold them, as we hold the rest of mankind, Enemies in War, in Peace Friends.

We, therefore, the Representatives of the united States of America, in General Congress, Assembled, appealing to the Supreme Judge of the world for the rectitude of our intentions, do, in the Name, and by Authority of the good People of these Colonies, solemnly publish and declare, That these United Colonies are, and of Right ought to be Free and Independent States; that they are Absolved from all Allegiance to the British Crown, and that all political connection between them and the State of Great Britain, is and ought to be totally dissolved; and that as Free and Independent States, they have full Power to levy War, conclude Peace, contract Alliances, establish Commerce, and to do all other Acts and Things which Independent States may of right do. — And for the support of this Declaration, with a firm reliance on the protection of divine Providence, we mutually pledge to each other our Lives, our Fortunes and our sacred Honor.

John Hancock

Button Gwinnett
Lyman Hall
Geo Walton.

Wm Hooper
Joseph Hewes,
John Penn

Edward Rutledge.
Thos Heyward Junr.
Thomas Lynch Junr.
Arthur Middleton

Samuel Chase
Wm Paca
Thos Stone
Charles Carroll of Carrollton

George Wythe
Richard Henry Lee
Th Jefferson
Benja Harrison
Thos Nelson jr.
Francis Lightfoot Lee
Carter Braxton

Robt Morris
Benjamin Rush
Benja Franklin
John Morton
Geo Clymer
Jas Smith
Geo Taylor
James Wilson
Geo Ross
Caesar Rodney
Geo Read
Tho McKean

Wm Floyd
Phil. Livingston
Frans Lewis
Lewis Morris

Richd Stockton
Jno Witherspoon
Fras Hopkinson
John Hart
Abra Clark

Josiah Bartlett
Wm Whipple
Saml Adams
John Adams
Robt Treat Paine
Elbridge Gerry
Step Hopkins
William Ellery
Roger Sherman
Samel Huntington
Wm Williams
Oliver Wolcott
Matthew Thornton

THE DECISION IS MADE

HISTORICAL SOCIETY OF PENNSYLVANIA

On July 4, 1776, the Continental Congress, meeting in Independence Hall, solemnly voted that the Declaration of Independence be adopted. Robert Edge Pine and Edward Savage painted the scene above in 1785, nine years after the historic occasion. The courageous signers dipped their pens in the three-piece silver inkstand (right), still to be seen where they used it.

INDEPENDENCE NATIONAL HISTORICAL PARK, PHILADELPHIA

By mid-July most Americans had seen copies of the Declaration or heard it read in public. Above, an 18th-century print shows such a reading, and the listening crowd's reaction.

OVERLEAF: Parades, picnics, toasts, patriotic songs and declamations, fireworks—all these typical Fourth of July celebrations are seen in this 1819 painting by J. L. Krimmel.

CHAPTER 8

COCKPIT OF BATTLE

Military operations of some significance began before the signing of the Declaration of Independence on July 4, 1776. In the fall of 1775, the Americans invaded Canada, and on the last day of the year Generals Benedict Arnold and Richard Montgomery made an attack upon Quebec. Arnold, personally leading 650 of the men, moved past the gates and into the city, where he was met by gunfire that wounded a number of his soldiers and left a bullet in his own leg. Daniel Morgan, another of the American officers, found himself engaged in heavy street fighting and made the fatal mistake of holding up, waiting for assistance from Montgomery, who had been killed. The British counterattacked at this point, and house by house they drove back the Americans, forcing some to surrender and others to retreat. The price of the abortive assault was about 100 killed or wounded and perhaps 400 taken prisoner. With Arnold wounded and Montgomery dead, the campaign

The American leader Richard Montgomery dies during the 1775 attack on Quebec, in a detail from a John Trumbull painting.

was practically over. But the British, because of a raging snowstorm, did not take up a serious pursuit of the defeated remnants, nor did they drive the Americans out of Canada until the following spring. Although the thrust at Quebec was unsuccessful, it served to deter aggressive British moves from that direction at a critical time in the war. A large body of troops coming to America from England was diverted for the future defense of Quebec. To some Americans, however, the virtual destruction of a 5,000-man army and the large expenditure of money were a high price to pay for this kind of respite.

Patriots who read the discouraging news of failure at Quebec found solace in the dispatches from Boston. On the morning of March 26, 1776, Sir William Howe moved his army and about 1,000 Tory sympathizers out of that city. They sailed for Halifax, Nova Scotia, glad to be freed from the threatening American guns that peered down upon them from Dorchester Heights. During his confinement in Boston, Howe had pondered over ways to bring the colonial upstarts to heel. At first he thought a modest army, properly led, would do the job, but as time passed and reports of growing rebel strength came in, he gradually raised his estimates of the required number to about 20,000. New York, he decided, was the focal point, and after it was secured, the Hudson River would provide the means of driving a great wedge between New England and the other colonies.

The Southern campaign

The grand plan of divide and conquer would take time, particularly in view of the delays that Howe was encountering as he tried to refurbish his army at Halifax. New York was spared for the moment, while the Southern colonies absorbed the next British blows. As early as mid-1775, strategists across the Atlantic had convinced themselves and the king that only a few regulars were needed to bolster the loyalists from Virginia southward. Accordingly, in January, 1776, Sir Henry Clinton sailed from Boston with an expeditionary force, intending to join the loyalists at Cape Fear, North Carolina, from where the assault would be made. But before Clinton arrived, Governor Josiah Martin, too eager and confident, gave the word to attack, only to see his supporters instantly crushed by Colonel James Moore's militiamen. Those who fled, leaving behind their dead or wounded, were run down and captured, and Carolina's loyalist forces lost another 900 men.

Martin's precipitous action upset Clinton's plans, but after being joined by troops from England under Lord Cornwallis—with the support of Sir Peter Parker, whose fleet was anchored off Cape Fear—Clinton decided to try to take South Carolina and set out for Charleston. Congress, well aware that the slow-moving force was bound for a port of such importance, sought to prevent its capture. This busy harbor, perhaps the most vital along the Southern coastline, was a main base for privateers as well as a center of trade, and its loss would be serious. General Charles Lee was assigned to defend the Southern Department and hurried to his new post.

Colonel William Moultrie, a South Carolinian, was already preparing Charleston's defense, particularly the redoubts of Fort Moultrie on Sullivan's Island, which the invaders would have to pass to attack the city. Lee's demands that Moultrie abandon the fort, on the ground that it provided no avenue of retreat, and Moultrie's flat refusal to obey demonstrated an early conflict between central and state authority. When the British fleet appeared and bombarded Fort Moultrie for 12 hours, only to withdraw, leaving Charleston unscathed, it probably saved Moultrie some embarrassment. And Lee's mood must have become forgiving when he learned that a shot from shore had caught Admiral Parker in the posterior, tearing off the seat of his breeches and carrying away a patch of titled hide. Between the futility of the attack and Parker's

Benedict Arnold began his 350-mile march from Boston to Quebec with 1,100 men. He lost half to cold and hunger as he went through the wilds of Maine.

wounded dignity, the British decided to call it a day. Back to New York went Clinton, ready to aid Howe but determined to capture Charleston ultimately. Four years later he would.

Taking New York in 1776

To the British, New York was of more strategic importance than a city like Charleston, and with this the Americans agreed. Of the 25,000 residents in the spring of 1776, more than 10,000 labored to make Manhattan Island a graveyard for British landing forces. General Washington dispersed his forces among other islands in the harbor, determined to hold Manhattan at all costs. When, on July 2, 1776, Howe landed 10,000 men on Staten Island, there was no resistance, nor was there opposition as he built up his force to more than 30,000 in the following weeks. The Americans prepared their own defenses, hoping that an assault would be made as it had been at Breed's Hill, where the entrenched had the advantage. By mid-August they were getting restless,

211

Colonel William Moultrie (above), commander of the fort on Sullivan's Island outside of Charleston, gave the Americans a great victory in 1776 when his men withstood the attack of 10 British ships (right).

however, for the plodding, cautious Howe still had not made his move.

Because he wanted to winter his men on Manhattan, Howe was eager to capture it without unnecessary destruction. Yet until he forced the American artillery out of Brooklyn Heights, on Long Island, the city across the East River would be untenable for him. When he sent troops ashore on Long Island, there was again no resistance, as the Americans waited on the Heights. But the British had learned something in Boston, and this time they refused to fall into the trap. Instead of the main roads, they took ones that had been left

unguarded. The woods around the Heights were thick with American riflemen, ready to shoot down the British and their Hessian mercenaries. But they never got the chance, for they were outflanked and struck savagely from behind. In panic they fled, and their pursuers pinned them to trees with bayonets as they futilely tried to reload their long rifles. Yet Washington got his men out of the near-disastrous situation and back to Manhattan, under cover of a heavy

fog, because Howe did not follow up his advantage.

The respite was brief. During the next two months, British pressure against Manhattan forced another retreat, this time across the Hudson River into New Jersey. To Howe's frustration, Washington refused to be cornered or maneuvered into a showdown fight. Such evasive tactics might prevent complete defeat, but as the Americans fell back toward the Delaware River, desertions ran high and the army shrank as if it had suffered heavy losses in battle. Washington was now in command of only about 3,000 discouraged men.

The first victories

Howe, always slow to move, this time did not bother to give personal pursuit. New York society and his low regard for Washington's raggle-taggle army prompted him to turn over the chase to Cornwallis, who quickly sent the Americans flying into

Pennsylvania. Philadelphia was now vulnerable, and on December 12, Congress, fearful of capture, fled, to take up temporary quarters at Baltimore. Only two days before, Congress had issued resolutions expressing great confidence in the cause and enjoining its supporters to stand firm in these critical hours. Philadelphia was not a great military base, but the damage its capture would have upon American morale was incalculable. Washington was now faced with the necessity of gaining even a small success, for clearly the military and political situation was deteriorating. Such was the background for his now-famous crossing of the Delaware River on Christmas night. He attacked the celebration-spent Hessian mercenaries at Trenton, New Jersey, early the following morning. The casualties were low, about 30 British and five Americans, but the total of prisoners ran to about 900 men and officers. To raise the spirits of the Philadelphians—and all Americans—Washington marched his Hessian prisoners through the streets of Philadelphia, and almost precipitated a riot among the citizenry, who wanted prompt revenge. The action at Trenton was no more than a raid—the American troops drank too much of their booty to keep on fighting—but it indicated to both sides that the ragged rebels had not yet given up.

Washington now had to prove to the enemy—and to his countrymen—that the successful attack upon the sleepy Hessians had been more than a

It was on Christmas night, 1776, that Washington made his historic crossing of the Delaware River, as visualized in this painting by Emanuel Leutze. The weather was fiercely cold, with gale-driven sleet hitting the boats. At four in the morning, the army still had nine miles to march to Trenton in order to surprise the British at dawn.

215

piece of luck. As the British were literally up in arms over the defeat and were out in numbers to avenge it, the Americans had to strike fast and in some unexpected spot. Once again Washington slipped out of camp, leaving fires burning brightly to deceive the British, and made for Princeton. Here he smashed the defending troops, and then went into camp at Morristown, not more than 25 miles from Howe's forces in New Brunswick.

American victories at Trenton and Princeton did not greatly discourage the British military leaders in America, but in England there was much dissatisfaction with the way the war was going. After a long and careful preparation, Howe and his subordinates were ready to resume their campaign in the spring of 1777, with every hope that this would be the final year of fighting. Despite Washington's efforts at training and regrouping during the early months of 1777, his army was only about 4,000 men. Such a force did not promise serious resistance to mounting numbers of troops arriving from England. Soon the imbalance of numbers must have its effect, reasoned Howe, and the insurrection would come to an end.

Burgoyne (left) surrenders to Gates (center) at Saratoga, offering him his sword. Gates returned it, invited him to dinner. Painting by John Trumbull.

Dividing the colonies

Holding to the original plan of dividing the colonies and subduing them one by one, the British now proposed to send about 7,700 men under General John "Gentleman Johnny" Burgoyne from Quebec to Albany, by way of Lake Champlain. Howe would then send a force from New York City to meet him, thus closing the nutcracker on the Americans. Lord Germain, colonial secretary, had made it a practice to cut Howe's requests for men and supplies, but in his enthusiasm for the new campaign, he was lavish in his support of Burgoyne's army. The campaign was so widely publicized that even the Americans knew all about it. Down out of Canada marched the British, striking the Americans hard at Ticonderoga, where they won decisively. Confident now, with his splendidly equipped troops and his brilliantly hued Indian allies as outriders, Burgoyne pressed on toward Albany, where he hoped to join Howe's forces.

Howe did not share Germain's high optimism for Burgoyne's campaign. He had no objection to a pincers movement and in fact had long advocated it, but he was annoyed because Burgoyne had received reinforcements that Howe himself wanted. Lured by reports of loyalist strength in Pennsylvania, he moved his army there from New York in July, 1777, determined to strike a master blow that would split the colonies in two and end the war. With elaborate caution he approached Philadelphia, denied to him the year before, hoping to crush Washington's army while he captured the city. But try as he would, Howe could not catch the elusive Washington or lure him into battle, and the lost time foreclosed the possibility of joining Burgoyne up the Hudson River.

By September, Burgoyne approached Albany, where General Horatio Gates awaited him in a strong defensive position on the banks of the Hudson. Burgoyne's forces had dwindled. Several hundred of his men had been left behind to guard Fort Ticonderoga; another 800 had been lost in a sharp action at Bennington, Vermont. Only about 6,500 remained. Meanwhile, word sped across the countryside of Burgoyne's progress, and as he drew on, American militiamen —ill-equipped and variously armed— appeared from everywhere. By the end of September, they outnumbered the British about three to one.

The fall rains turned roads into mire, and Burgoyne's army bogged down. Nevertheless, he attacked, believing it to be his only hope, as each day increased the disparity in size of the two armies. In a series of actions around Saratoga, in which the Americans counterattacked heavily, the British lost some 1,200 men. Failing to get the expected support from Howe, and unable to retreat, Burgoyne surrendered his entire force, still nearly 5,500 strong. He tried to take some of the sting out of the defeat by calling his capitulation a "convention"—a condition of which was that his men, after pledging they would not again serve in the American campaign, would be marched to Boston and given passage home. Burgoyne's suspicions were aroused by the alacrity with which Gates accepted this condition, but there was nothing he could do but sign and take his chances. He lost his gamble, for Congress refused to support the promise of parole and held the prisoners on this side of the Atlantic until the war's end.

Climax

The victory at Saratoga by the Continental Army prevented the British from driving a wedge between the colonies. And it showed that American troops could beat British troops. The French observed this battle with particular interest—as they had observed Washington's defeats in 1777 at Brandywine Creek and at Germantown in Pennsylvania, and the British settling down for the winter in Philadelphia. Historians argue over how much influence Saratoga had on the French decision to aid America, but no one denies that it had some. It now appeared that the Americans had a better-than-even chance to win their war. More than that, France knew the British were in a conciliatory mood,

ready to offer attractive peace terms. If this happened, the British would be strong again. After weighing these considerations, the French invited Benjamin Franklin and Silas Deane to a conference. During February and March, 1778, arrangements were worked out whereby France and the American colonies would make common cause against England. It was agreed that neither would make a separate peace with the enemy. Along with the war treaty, another was made

In the battle of Germantown, Wayne and Sullivan lead the American forces, in the background, against the British, who took refuge in the Chew House (right). The 1782 painting is by Xavier Della Gatta.

VALLEY FORGE HISTORICAL SOCIETY

220

between France and America, providing for commercial friendship and cooperation. The importance of the French alliance is hard to overestimate. Without it, the outcome of the American Revolution might have been far different.

In June, 1778, France formally entered the war on the American side. The next year, Spain joined as an ally of France. In 1780, England went to war with the Netherlands. A League of Armed Neutrality was formed. Its members—Russia, Denmark, Sweden, the Netherlands, Prussia, Portugal, Austria, and the Kingdom of the Two Sicilies—were tired of England's interpretations of her privileges on the seas and were ready to fight. Englishmen began to lose interest in the American conflict. With France, Spain, and the Netherlands at war with her, with an armed league bristling with threats, and with military reverses across the Atlantic, England asked for negotiations.

In 1778, even before Spain had joined France against England, five commissioners had been appointed by Parliament to talk with the Americans about a settlement. They had been empowered to offer almost anything—except independence. The Earl of Carlisle, who headed the mission, had been obliged to report to Parliament that the Americans were not interested in his terms. Now, in 1780, a French army of 5,000 veterans, ready to fight alongside their allies, reached Rhode Island. The British, who still hoped to negotiate, nevertheless continued their military efforts, and turned again toward the Southern states. Trying to drive a wedge there, they succeeded in cutting off Georgia. And in May, 1780, they captured Charleston. Gates was dispatched to drive them out, but he was roundly defeated.

Before long, however, Americans had better news. Cornwallis, hoping to lead his troops through Virginia and cut the colonies in two, landed a large force at Yorktown on the York River. By August, 1781, with French naval forces blocking his retreat by sea, and French and American soldiers surrounding his fortifications, he was cornered. On October 19, he surrendered his entire army of 7,000 men, and the British government, thor-

oughly discouraged by the turn of events, hastened to sue for peace.

The naval war

While American land forces struggled against the enemy on the battlefield, and public lethargy at home, a young and untried navy did its best to cope with overwhelming odds at sea. Its beginnings were as informal as those of the Continental Army, of which the colonies' first armed vessels were a part. But in the fall of 1775, Congress decided that naval warfare should be under the control of the Marine, or Naval, Committee. A sum of $100,000 was appropriated for the outfitting and manning of ships. To encourage enlistment, men and officers were promised half the profits from captured prizes.

The regular navy was never large. It consisted of about 40 deep-water "principal ships," plus a smaller num-

On October 17, 1781, exactly four years after Burgoyne's surrender at Saratoga, Cornwallis wrote to Washington asking for a cease-fire, "to settle terms for the surrender of the posts of York and Gloucester." Frenchman Louis Van Blarenberghe, an eyewitness at Yorktown, painted the long, thin column of white-uniformed French troops marching into the siege lines around Yorktown as officers (center) make plans.

The British Serapis *(right) is raked by the* Bonhomme Richard *during the battle fought in 1779 by John Paul Jones (above).*

ber in the fresh-water fleet on the Great Lakes. By the end of the war, only three first-line vessels remained; the others had all been sunk or captured. American privateers, with their rapierlike thrusts at British commerce, were the most effective sea force. Through his daring exploits, which included raids on England and Ireland, John Paul Jones became the hero of this war. The battle between his *Bonhomme Richard* (named in honor of Benjamin Franklin) and the British *Serapis* was to become a highlight in American naval legend. Although Jones lost his own ship, he captured the *Serapis* and sailed it into a French port. Through the efforts of Jones, Captain John Barry, and others, some 200 enemy vessels were taken. Besides crippling the British fleet, the Americans got from these

prizes some $6,000,000 worth of much-needed supplies. The harassment at sea was long remembered by Great Britain, and Americans were to use the same weapon to advantage again in their next war with her.

Peace at any price

Before Yorktown, it is doubtful if the Americans could have had peace without allowing the British to retain the territory they had already captured. The royal navy held most of the important seaports from New York to Savannah. But Yorktown was such a blow that Lord North resigned in despair. George III wrote a statement of abdication, thought better of it, and asked Lord Rockingham to form a new government and try for peace. With men friendly to the Americans in control, the official British attitude changed. When Benjamin Franklin was approached in Paris, he sensed that his position was much improved and stipulated complete independence, including return of captured territory. (He also blandly asked for all of Canada, suggesting that American ownership would prevent later difficulties, but the request was later dropped.)

Lord Shelburne, who became prime minister in July, 1782, was a statesman of vision and willing to negotiate. The American commissioners proceeded to deal with him—despite their promise to the French that they would not sign a separate peace—and on November 30, 1782, terms were agreed upon. A proviso was included that the treaty would not go into effect until England and France signed articles of peace. When that was done, in January, 1783, the American Revolution was in reality over.

The terms of the final treaty, signed September 3, 1783, refute the 20th-century belief that America never lost a war or won a peace. The young nation gained its freedom, and lands east of the Mississippi River as well. Thanks to the wily New Englander, John Adams, fishing rights in Canadian waters, previously granted to the colonies, were retained. The British further promised not to carry off any American property when they evacuated their forces, and asked in return that debts owed to British subjects by Americans be paid. Our commissioners said they would recommend payment and not hinder collection—an evasively vague commitment, as later developments proved.

With the war over, the peace signed, and George III on record as having said good riddance, the Americans were free to embark upon the seas of independence. The next few years were to indicate that the waters of freedom are often choppy and the responsibility of operating the ship of state much greater than can be foreseen. But, for better or for worse, the colonials had struck out for themselves; now they would have only themselves to answer to for future mistakes. This was the way they wanted it.

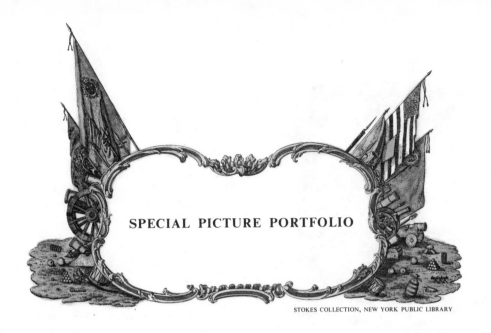

THE ARMS
AND THE MEN

The American Revolution was an 18th-century war, fought in the style of that time. The battlefields were cloaked in the smoke of cannons, the air heavy with the sharp smell of black powder. Drums beat as the troops advanced, and the neighing of wounded horses filled the air. The colonials were ill-prepared at the start, fighting without experienced officers, organization, ammunition, or uniforms, but they gained experience and equipment as battle followed battle. Fortunately, they began their revolt when Britain's military commitments overseas were already high and her supply of adequately trained manpower was low. But the British, with their long tradition of military excellence and superior equipment, were still formidable enemies. The Revolution was an infantryman's war, and this gave the colonials another advantage: They were defending their own country and fighting in their own fields, while most of the British troops were strangers to the land. Although the American infantryman was not so well trained in the manual of arms as the British, he had usually hunted for his livelihood in frontier country and could handle a rifle or musket well. Moreover, he often carried his own familiar weapons into battle. By the end of the war the American army had improved its organization and effectiveness, but it soon dispersed, the farmers and merchants returning to their occupations. Created for a specific purpose, there was no longer any need for it to remain active.

227

GUILFORD COURTHOUSE NATIONAL MILITARY PARK

MARCH TO BATTLE

Both British and American troops marched into the battles of the Revolution to the rhythm of drums like the one at the left.

As *Recruiting Serjeant,* the satirical drawing at the right illustrates, the British found it hard to get good recruits.

The flintlock musket was the standard infantry weapon in the Revolution. The drawings below, published in a British drill manual, show (1) the musket, (2) the bayonet being affixed, (3) the musket being primed and loaded, (4) the bayonet charge, and (5) the musket being fired.

1

2

3

4   5

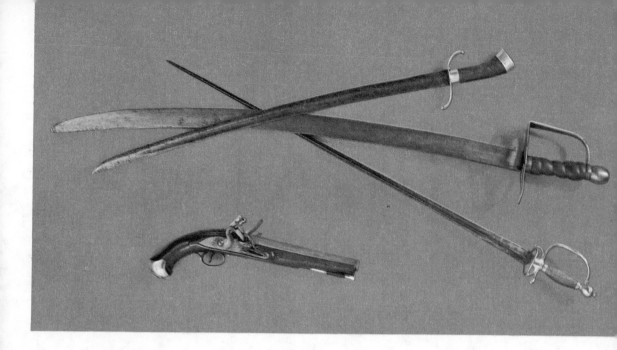

Swords and pistols were used in the Revolution as well as muskets. The British pistol was carried by a cavalryman. The hunting sword (top) and the small sword (bottom) were carried by officers; the heavy weapon at center is a cavalry saber.

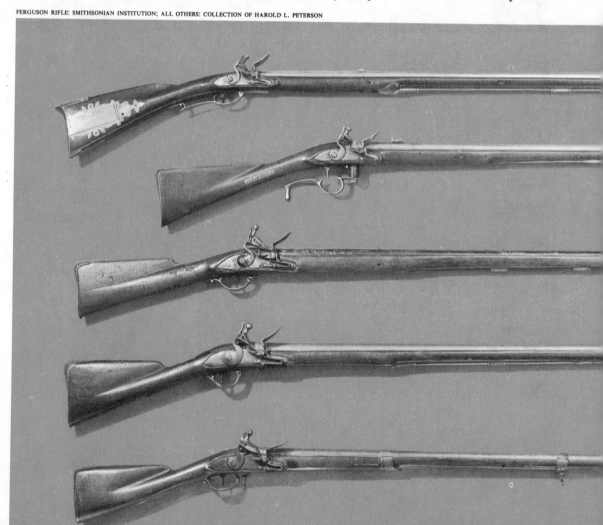

THE INSTRUMENTS OF WAR

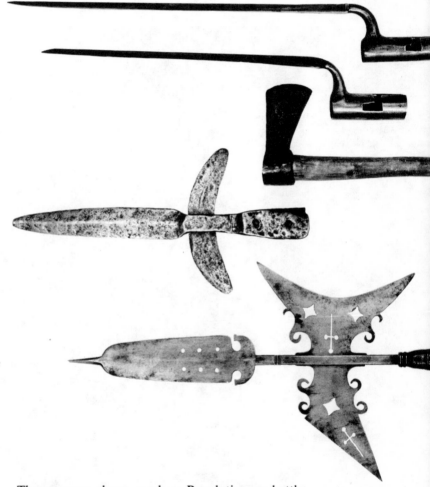

The weapons above, used on Revolutionary battle-fields, are (top to bottom) bayonets, a tomahawk, a spontoon, and a halberd. Tomahawks were carried by American troops; spontoons on poles were used in charges; and the halberd was a symbol of rank.

Rifles and muskets of the Revolution (left, top to bottom) are the American rifle (also called the Kentucky rifle or the Pennsylvania rifle), the Ferguson rifle, a Committee of Safety musket, a Brown Bess musket, and a French infantry musket.

231

CANNON
AND MORTAR

The drawings of cannon and mortar below were published in Muller's *Treatise of Artillery*. Above is a cannon drawn by Charles W. Peale in his diary.

232

So desperate was the colonists' need for cannon that 59 were dragged by oxen
through the snow from the captured British fort at Ticonderoga to Boston.

WEST POINT MUSEUM, FORT TICONDEROGA MUSEUM, WASHINGTON'S HEADQUARTERS AND MUSEUM, COLLECTION OF H. CHARLES MCBARRON—PHOTO, ARNOLD NEWMAN

THE ARMS AND THE MEN

A SOLDIER'S GEAR

Assembled here are uniforms and equipment of American infantrymen, including canteen, pipe, money, maps, and red blanket roll. The coat, buff vest, and pants, buckled shoes, and plumed cap (far right) were worn by the Continental Corps of Light Infantry in 1780. The infantryman carried the French musket with bayonet (top), and he made his own cartridge for it from paper, black powder, and lead ball (on vest). The rifleman wore a spun linen shirt and tricorn hat (far left) and carried a powder horn, lead balls, and shot pouch (on shirt) instead of cartridges; riflemen also carried tomahawks (top).

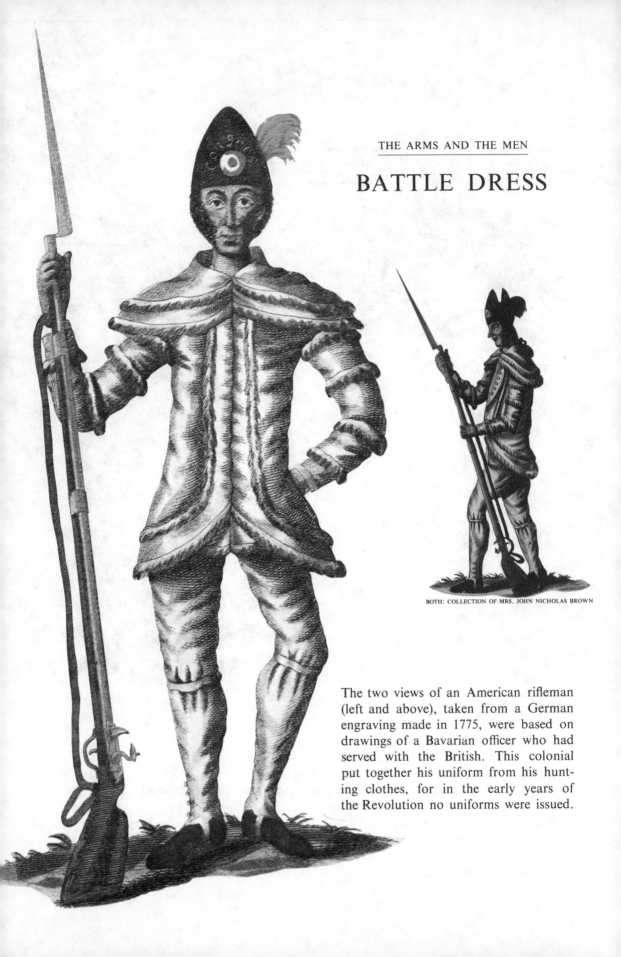

BATTLE DRESS

BOTH: COLLECTION OF MRS. JOHN NICHOLAS BROWN

The two views of an American rifleman (left and above), taken from a German engraving made in 1775, were based on drawings of a Bavarian officer who had served with the British. This colonial put together his uniform from his hunting clothes, for in the early years of the Revolution no uniforms were issued.

The Continental Army eventually acquired regulation dress (left), purchased in France and adopted toward the end of the Revolution.

The appearance of the rebel rifleman (right) is caricatured by a British artist.

Some American rebels dressed like those in the engraving below. Many Continentals, the German artist had been told, were barefoot.

REGIMENTAL FLAG, 5TH FOOT

HIS MAJESTY'S ARMY

REGIMENTAL FLAG, 33RD FOOT

COLLECTION OF MRS. JOHN NICHOLAS BROWN

REGIMENTAL FLAG, 9TH FOOT

ALL FLAGS: NEW YORK PUBLIC LIBRARY

Wherever the British army went, it took its historic uniforms and ancient traditions. The man at the right is an 18th-century grenadier officer; to his right is a drummer boy in full dress.

The British army established many camps in the colonies like the one below. These tent cities were laid out in a traditional pattern and were run according to a long-established set of regulations, enforced by experienced career officers.

BRITISH MUSEUM, LONDON

AID FROM ABROAD

The Continental Army eagerly enlisted the support of Europeans. King Louis XVI of France sent four superbly trained and equipped infantry regiments to fight beside the rebels. They were dressed like the men in the print by an 18-century French artist (opposite). Rochambeau, the general the French sent to America, is shown drilling his troops in the cartoon above, by the British artist Thomas Colley, which makes fun of the elegant soldiers.

The German soldier at the left was one of the 30,000 German mercenaries who fought for the British in the colonies. As many of the men were from the state of Hesse-Kassel, they were called Hessians.

COLLECTION OF MRS. JOHN NICHOLAS BROWN

N.. SOISSONNOIS.
LIMOSIN . BRETAGNE.

THE BATTLE OF PRINCETON

One of the great American victories of the Revolution was the defeat of the British in Princeton on January 3, 1777. This view of the battle was painted by the son of the American general, Hugh Mercer, who was mortally wounded there. George Washington (on horseback, left center) is directing American cannon fire with his sword. The British army is massed beyond the fence at the far right. In the first state of the battle, fought in William Clark's orchard south of Princeton, the advance guard of the Americans met British troops headed toward Trenton to join General Cornwallis. The British were winning the confused melee—until Washington arrived with the main force of his American troops and succeeded in forcing the British to retreat to New Brunswick.

Painted in the early 1800s by John A. Woodside of Philadelphia, this patriotic
composition expresses the feelings of the new nation's youthful independence.

CHAPTER 9

Revolution Within

During the war years, the sound and fury of battle reflected the more dramatic, overt aspects of the American Revolution. Equally significant was the revolution taking place at the same time in the political, social, and economic life of the new Americans. Slave trade and inheritance laws, penal codes and education for all—these were just a few of the matters under discussion in state legislatures. Eighteenth-century liberalism helped to germinate seeds of liberty and democracy; the Revolution was the hothouse that nurtured them. Only when the fighting was over, and their independence won, did Americans begin to sense that a new nation had been created.

In the years between the settling of Jamestown and the signing of the Declaration of Independence, the colonial tasted independence and found he liked it. To achieve self-determination, and freedom from the mother country, he reluctantly joined in a common fight, waged by a loose confederation of states. To this confederation he gave only mild allegiance; his strong loyalty was to his own state. The ardently patriotic New Yorker or Virginian seemed hardly aware that what had influenced him might have had the same effect on his neighbor. Each state regarded itself defiantly and proudly as a separate, self-sufficient entity, and had no intention of relinquishing the sovereignty it was struggling to wrest from England to a strong central government, even if it helped form it. One by one, each state set about establishing its own government.

The colony becomes a state

The people, as John Adams said, wanted "a standing law to live by." This demand of the American for written law had its beginnings many years before. Colonies had been founded under written charters; they had been governed by them through the colonial years. With faith that their cause would triumph, 11 of the 13 colonies put their most respected citizens to drafting a constitution for their state, which they expected to be the supreme law of the land.

What were the sources of these state constitutions? What influenced them? In what way were they alike? From the 18th-century political theorists, such as John Locke, the constitution-makers adapted the fundamental yet revolutionary belief that all power is derived from the people, who will govern themselves through duly appointed representatives or officials. (And to safeguard their republican governments, the constitutions provided checks and balances.) From England, the constitution-makers borrowed the common law, under which the colonists had lived for many years. They also retained many elements of colonial political institutions, all of which had originally derived from British forms of government. Out of this common background

Samuel Adams, painted by John Singleton Copley, was a member of the Massachusetts constitutional convention held in 1780.

of ideals and political experience, each state drew up a constitution that was, as we shall see, much like that of its neighbor.

In detail, the constitutions varied widely. For example, Virginia's, drafted in 1776, had features familiar to modern Americans. It had three parts—a Bill of Rights, a Declaration of Independence, and a Frame of Government. In good Jeffersonian language, the document stated that all men are created equal, and all power is derived from the people, who can change their form of government when they change their minds. The Frame of Government, containing 21 parts, set up a bicameral legislature and provided for the election of a governor by joint ballot of both houses.

Pennsylvania's constitution, also drafted in 1776, was more radical. It was fathered by Benjamin Franklin, but those who deeply feared executive power apparently gained control of the convention. The legislature was to be a single house; every free man who had lived and paid taxes in Pennsylvania for a year could vote; an executive council ruled in place of a governor. The supremacy of the legislative branch was emphasized by the ruling that the executive council could not veto any act of the legislature. This did not mean that the legislators could run free, however. A council of censors, elected every seven years, was to see to it that the constitution was not violated. Although they could not actually annul laws, they were empowered to request a constitutional convention to amend the constitution, and this power was an impressive deterrent to unruly legislators.

The Massachusetts constitution, drafted in 1780, is probably the best example of a deliberate transition from colony to commonwealth. With minor modifications it is still the fundamental law of that state. Until 1780, Massachusetts had been governed by its provincial charter. When the people learned that the General Court (a legislative body) intended to draw up a new state constitution, they objected. People from Concord, for example, were reluctant to trust the legislature with anything so important; they recommended a constitutional convention. When the General Court, ignoring the objections, issued a constitution proposed by its own members, five-sixths of the voters said no. Smarting under the defeat, the General Court had to call a convention.

At the convention, a committee that included John Adams was appointed to draft a new constitution. Its work was accepted and adopted on March 2, 1780. Elaborate safeguards to protect the individual were included. Here, unlike Pennsylvania, men of substance were powerful enough to make sure that radical democracy was not triumphant. Relatively high property qualifications for voting and officeholding guaranteed that the "right" people would rule.

The constitutions reveal, like all compacts resulting from compromise,

Jefferson contributed to Virginia's constitution. Painted by Rembrandt Peale.

the conflict between the far left and the far right. Usually the conservatives were able to get an early advantage, and the most influential members of society saw to it that their property interests were protected.

In Pennsylvania the middle classes and the frontiersmen gained control of the revolutionary movement, and as a result the constitution was liberal. Western Pennsylvanians won equal representation with the eastern Pennsylvanians, something not accomplished in all states. In Virginia, where the conservatives were able to dominate the liberals, the constitution was middle-of-the-road. South Carolina's, drafted in 1778, was so conservative that it made Virginia's look liberal. It

James Wilson, member of the Pennsylvania convention in 1776 and the Continental Congress, believed that the sovereignty of a government must reside in the people.

limited suffrage to men owning at least 50 acres of land. To hold office, a man had to have much more: A senator had to be worth at least 2,000 pounds, a governor had to have 10,000. Because of loose voting regulations, rich Charleston residents could be elected to represent areas in which they held land. Thus, about one-fifth of the people in South Carolina ruled the other four-fifths. The wealthy coastal planters were a stronghold of conservatism that dominated South Carolina through the Civil War.

Land the equalizer

Property qualifications did not, however, create a strong ruling class. Tradesmen and artisans who lived in towns usually had to suffer second-class citizenship. But most of the dominant group—90% of them—lived by tilling the soil. Farmers with little or no land could reasonably expect to become substantial property owners. The war itself brought about a tremendous turnover in ownership. With the restrictions of 1763 invalidated, the colonial had access to the limitless acres beyond the Appalachians. Along the Atlantic seaboard, land from individual and crown holdings was redistributed.

Proprietary landholders suffered under the revolutionaries. Pennsylvania helped itself to the unassigned lands of the Penn family, valued at about 1,000,000 pounds, granting the family only 130,000 pounds "in remembrance of the enterprising spirit of the founder." In Maryland the "remembrance" was a mere 10,000 pounds, so small that the British government later contributed an additional 90,000 pounds. The holdings of Lord Thomas Fairfax in Virginia, 5,000,000 acres, were confiscated by the state after his death in 1781.

Loyalists were deprived of their

holdings in all possible ways. Some large private estates, abandoned by Tories, were divided and sold. As the Revolution dragged on, the bitterness of the patriots increased. By 1778, wholesale confiscation of property was common. The loyalists were fined for evading military duty, for harboring the enemy, and for countless minor infractions. They were taxed unreasonably. Although forced to accept rents in depreciated Continental currency, they had to pay their own expenses and debts with hard money. In South Carolina and New York they were held responsible for robberies in their neighborhoods. The high point came in November, 1777, when the Continental Congress suggested that the states sell the property held by those believed to be loyal to the king and invest the money in Continental loan certificates. Within three years every state but South Carolina had.

In these ways, more and more land fell into the hands of patriots, many

More and more in the late years of the 18th century, emigrants moved along the Great Philadelphia Wagon Road and other trails leading west, filling the Appalachian slopes with farms like this one. Painted in 1845 by Edward Hicks.

of whom had never owned any before. Here we see the Revolution in a more revolutionary light. It had begun as a civil war between two parts of the Empire, but it developed into a political and economic struggle between the ruling class and the newly emerging class. The landed aristocracy lost much of its power as the new land-owners expressed their will at the ballot box. At a stroke they were elevated socially, politically, and economically. They did not mind paying taxes instead of quitrents, for they expected in return, and got, services from the state.

As the new land titles deluged the earlier aristocrats, their position was gradually washed away. Jefferson himself led the assault upon such feudal vestiges as the laws designed to preserve estates intact, which forbade their division. Other states followed Virginia, and by 1800 all states but two had decreed that *all* heirs had to get a share of the property at the death of the owner. Thus primogeniture, which gave the entire holding to the oldest son, and entail, which forbade dividing an estate, were virtually outlawed. (In North Carolina, daughters could not inherit property when there were sons in the family. In New Jersey, daughters were allotted a half portion.) The attack upon land monopoly was so widespread that when the Frenchman Alexis de Tocqueville visited the United States in the 1830s, he commented that the radical inheritance laws were partially responsible for the existence of democracy. He maintained that keeping estates intact is necessary for an aristocracy.

Other equalizers

Land distribution was the core of the revolution within. It widened suffrage, which in turn enabled democratic-minded men to strike out at all kinds of social injustice.

In a number of states the Anglican Church had long stood as a symbol of British authority. It was the official dispenser of religious dogma—and worse, in the eyes of many, were the taxes levied upon all for its support. As early as 1776, the new state constitutions of Maryland and North Carolina took from the Anglican Church its privileges, and Virginia followed. Jefferson, who headed the fight, described it as "the severest in which I have ever been engaged." Other states, like New York, Georgia, and South Carolina, took a less direct approach. Freedom was granted to all sects, thus depriving the Anglican Church of its privileged position as the state church. It was left to compete with the others on equal terms. If it survived, the states had no particular objection. Such reforms were received with joy by such sects as the Baptists, who claimed they had been subjected to "spiritual tyranny" by both the Anglican Church and New England Congregationalism.

The increasing feeling that human slavery had no place in the new order began to grow strong. How could the

Daniel Boone leads a group of pioneers west through the mountain passage that was known as the Cumberland Gap. Painting is by George Caleb Bingham.

American trumpet about the rights of man when there were a half-million slaves in the 13 states? Patrick Henry, with his keen awareness of injustice, said, "I believe a time will come when an opportunity will be offered to abol-ish this lamentable evil." Nor was this Virginian the only one who objected. In 1774, the First Continental Congress heard discussions of slavery as a wrong that should be corrected, and it adopted a nonimportation agree-

251

The French Revolution began in 1789. In part inspired by what had taken place in America, it also resulted from the excesses of the French kings, such as in building the Palace of Versailles (right).

ment on slaves. That same year the legislature of Rhode Island recorded its sentiment that personal liberty was the right of all men, regardless of color. Some states actually passed legislation against the slave trade; others sought to undermine it with prohibitive duties.

Slavery was only one of the social problems under review. Imprisonment as a penalty for unpaid debts was abolished, and many an honest man who had become financially enmeshed was given the opportunity to redeem himself. The number of offenses punishable by death was sharply cut back. An interest in general education emerged, and Pennsylvania and Virginia worked to establish public schools. Again Jefferson led the fight in Virginia, contending that a certain amount of state-financed education should be available to all men. Himself a man of some means, he nevertheless opposed fervently an aristocracy based upon wealth.

The struggle for union

Common danger during the war was what moved the colonies toward confederation. But the concept of a United States of America had existed, however weakly, long before the Revolution. Political theorists and even

imperial administrators had cherished the dream of unity along the Atlantic frontier, but colonial jealousies had thus far prevented it. From time to time, events had drawn the colonies into thoughts of union. In 1643, Massachusetts, Plymouth, Connecticut, and New Haven had formed the New England Confederation. Again, in 1754, Benjamin Franklin drew up the

Albany Plan of Union, which would unite all the colonies (except Georgia and Nova Scotia) under one president general. Both efforts resulted from Indian problems. The Confederation was terminated in 1684; the Albany Plan of Union was rejected outright by the colonies as well as by the English government.

In July, 1775, Franklin presented the idea of union to the Continental Congress. At that time there was little talk of independence, and his plan made no mention of it. He recommended a United Colonies of North America, formed for friendship and common defense. Each colony would have jurisdiction within its own boundary, and a general congress would handle all external affairs.

Given broad powers, the congress would act in the interest of general welfare and would try to settle differences between individual colonies. Matters best handled jointly—postal services, the regulation of currency, the control of commerce— would fall within its province. Each member colony would be expected to help financially and would be represented in the congress according to its male population. In place of a head of state, the united colonies would be governed by a board of councilors.

Many agreed with Franklin that unity was necessary. A decade before, a Charleston resident had written, "There ought to be no New England men, no New Yorkers, etc., known on the continent, but all of us Americans." Patrick Henry said it another way in 1774: "Where are your landmarks, your boundaries of Colonies . . . I am not Virginian, but an American." Yet even as late as 1776, when the Declaration of Independence was being drawn up and a committee had been appointed to consider a national constitution, delegates to the Continental Congress were still contesting the merits of the tentative provision that the central government would arbitrate boundary disputes.

The suggestion that each state have a single vote, and yet be taxed according to population, aroused even more vigorous protest, especially from the Southerners. They did not want blacks counted for tax purposes, claiming that slaves were simply property and should

no more be taxed than sheep or cattle. (This debate was held within four weeks of the adoption of the Declaration of Independence, which proclaims the equality of men!)

Franklin opposed a single vote for each state, maintaining that each should be represented according to the size of its population. Others differed over the question of empowering the national government to control Western lands. Georgia, the least populated of the colonies, had the most extensive land claims. Pennsylvania, one of the largest colonies, had no claims beyond her charter limits.

It is not surprising that heated debates developed over such questions. Although Americans had proclaimed to the world that they were united, this union had come about through resistance to a common enemy. Was union necessary after the enemy had been defeated? Was it feasible or desirable? Only the most forward-looking Americans, it seemed, had committed themselves irrevocably to this dream of a united America.

Government by permission

The Continental Congress should have formulated a government in 1776. That year marked the high point of nationalistic spirit during the war, and at its apex was Congress, popular and respected. By 1777, when Congress approved the Articles of Confederation, it no longer enjoyed such prestige. Reluctance to accept centralized power had again surged, and

When Charles Willson Peale painted Benjamin Franklin in 1789, a year before his death, he and his country had seen revolution, independence, and—now—union.

the tide of nationalism now receded. As it was, the Articles of Confederation granted little sovereignty to the central government; herein lay their weakness. The states had reserved to themselves this requisite of an effective government. Until they agreed to relinquish at least part of it, they were participants in nothing more than a league of friendship.

The Articles, sent out to the states in the fall of 1777 for ratification, pledged "perpetual union" for common defense and for the general welfare, but it was hardly more than a hopeful sentiment. One outstanding weakness was that Congress was not granted taxing powers; this was reserved strictly to the states. Each of them was to contribute according to the valuation of its surveyed lands and buildings. Even worse, Congress was given no authority to enforce collection, and the central government was obliged to depend upon the good faith of each state. The central government could borrow money, but with such limited money-raising resources, it was certainly a poor loan risk.

These were not the only deficiencies. Foreign affairs were supposed to fall within the province of Congress, but it could make war or negotiate for peace only when nine of the states agreed. If states fell to bickering over boundaries or Western land claims, Congress could appoint a commission to arbitrate, but it was allotted no power to appropriate any land for the United States. In the years after 1781,

when the Articles of Confederation were ratified, and the United States began its experiment of constitutional government, Congressmen began to feel like mere observers, sent by their states to listen but forbidden to act. It is not surprising that the caliber of the members declined.

Although it is easy to criticize the Articles, the astute men who wrote our first constitution should be credited with a remarkable achievement: They outlined a government—whatever its lacks—that the defiant states would accept.

From the beginning its weaknesses were apparent. Attempts to get the Articles ratified brought out familiar jealousies. The main quarrel stemmed from five of the new states having definite Western limits while the others all had extensive claims beyond the mountains. New Jersey, New Hampshire, Delaware, Rhode Island, and Maryland feared that the states with land claims would become rich and powerful enough to swallow up the smaller members of the union.

Meanwhile, with the war still on, each state tended to continue its own fight with Great Britain, raiding its neighbors for men and resources when necessary, and hoarding its own strength. One can see the truth of James Madison's assertion that the newly formed federation was "nothing more than a treaty of amity, of commerce, and of alliance, between independent and sovereign states."

The Articles of Confederation indi-

Benjamin West's painting of the preliminary peace negotiations was unfinished because the British commissioners, who were to be on the right, refused to pose.

cate that the colonies had not yet achieved insight into the building of a nation. The extreme caution used in doling out power reflected the feeling that a jump to a supergovernment was both premature and dangerous. The outcome of the life-and-death struggle with Great Britain was still doubtful, and Americans were in no mood to pass from one yoke to another. Time would bring maturity to a new people. Before long the clumsiness of their government would be brought home to them, and necessity would once more be the mother of political invention.

MAIN TEXT CONTINUES IN VOLUME 4

Washington took leave of his officers at Fraunces Tavern on December 4, 1783, the same day that

the last British troops left Staten Island and Long Island. The painting is by Alonzo Chappel.

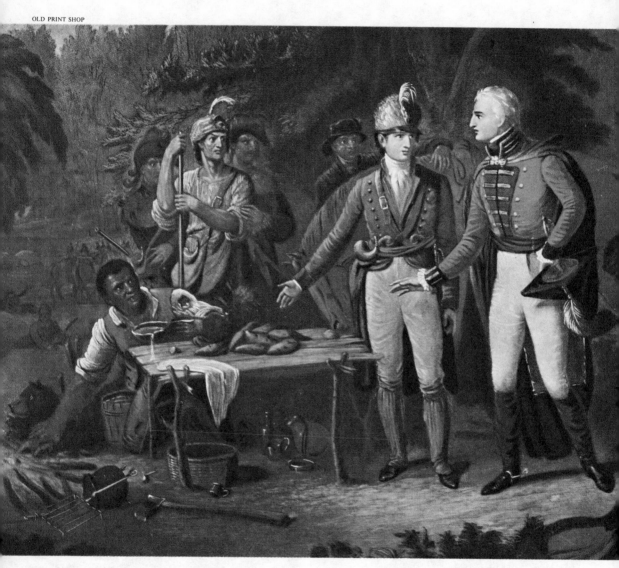

Francis Marion (center) offers his humble meal of baked potatoes to an amazed British officer. Legend says that the artist of the painting, John Blake White, remembered Marion's features from the time he sat on his knee as a child. But as is frequently the case with the stories about the general, the whole incident may be folklore. Nonetheless, the painting was used on Confederate currency during the Civil War.

Francis Marion:
The Elusive Swamp Fox

A SPECIAL CONTRIBUTION BY

GEORGE F. SCHEER

Guerrilla warfare in South Carolina swamps and surprise attacks upon enemy regiments made this colonial general and his band of men important in winning the young nation's victory.

> *Our band is few, but true and tried,*
> *Our leader frank and bold;*
> *The British soldier trembles*
> *When Marion's name is told.*

There is the poem, there is the sentence or two in schoolbooks, and there is the sobriquet, the Swamp Fox. That's about all anyone seems to remember about General Francis Marion—except, perhaps, that once he invited a British officer to dinner, in his camp under a flag of truce, and served only fire-baked potatoes on a bark slab and a beverage of vinegar and water. "But, surely, general," the officer said, "this cannot be your usual fare." "Indeed, sir, it is," Marion replied, "and we are fortunate on this occasion, entertaining company, to have more than our usual allowance." The visiting Briton is supposed to have been so impressed that he resigned his commission and returned to England, full of sympathy for the self-sacrificing American patriots. That's not exactly the way it happened, but that's the way it goes in the Marion legend.

The legend was the invention of a specialist in hero-making, the Reverend Mason Locke

Weems. He, with the help of one of Marion's devoted soldiers, Peter Horry, wrote the first life of the general, "a celebrated partizan officer in the Revolutionary War, against the British and Tories, in South Carolina and Georgia," drawn, according to the title page, "from documents furnished by his brother-in-arms, Brigadier General P. Horry." The sensational little book, a captivating melange of fact and much fiction, firmly established Francis Marion as the Robin Hood of the Revolution.

That first "biography" appeared in 1809, and the Marion of Parson Weems remains the Marion of American history. Yet when you piece together the surviving letters, the orderly books, the official reports, you come to realize that Marion's daring forays are not merely the romantic stuff of folk literature, but that they made a definite contribution to the British defeat in the South.

From the outbreak of the Revolution until the spring of 1780, Marion put in five useful, though relatively inactive, years as an officer of the Second South Carolina Continental Regiment. But it was as a relentless guerrilla who never let up on the British after they overran his state that he earned his significance in history. He was not the only partisan those hard times discovered, but he stayed in the field longer than any of the others and best understood and carried out the mission of the partisan. And although he won no tide-turning battles, he had more than a little to do with what General Nathanael Greene, commanding the Southern Department, called "flushing

261

the bird" that General Washington caught at Yorktown.

Marion was 48 at the time, "rather below the middle stature," one of his men recalled, "lean and swarthy. His body was well set, but his knees and ankles were badly formed . . . He had a countenance remarkably steady; his nose was aquiline, his chin projecting; his forehead was large and high, and his eyes black and piercing." It was the kind of face some men considered hard-visaged.

Marion was a man with the steady habits of a modest planter who had lived alone most of his life. He ate and drank abstemiously; his voice was light but low when he talked, and that was seldom.

Whether he fought his brigade mounted or afoot (he usually rode to the enemy and then fought as infantry), he was always in the front of the attacks that made his name a terror in the British and Tory camp. But he was not given to ferocious gesture. In fact, they say he drew his sword, a light dress weapon, so seldom that it rusted in its scabbard. It was not for personal conspicuousness in battle that his men remembered him, but for a quiet fearlessness, for sagacity and perseverance, and for never foolishly risking himself or the brigade.

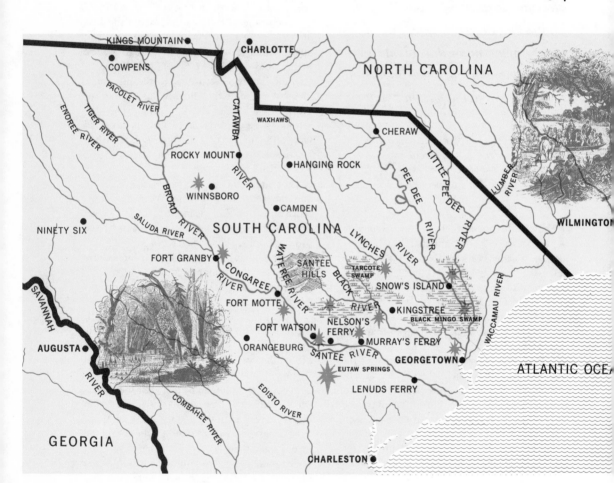

Marion's operations took place in a low, swampy region drained by many rivers, and after the Americans had been defeated at Camden, his followers represented the main colonial force in South Carolina. His major encounters with the British are marked in red.

They rode with confidence behind a man who never hesitated in the face of impossible odds to fight and run to live and fight another day. And he endeared himself to them when he slept with them on the ground, ate their fare, and endured fatigue and danger with the hardiest.

Marion's men actually had no official status. They were purely volunteers. When they came into the field, South Carolina was overrun by the British and their rebel government had evaporated. Of their own will, they took up arms to fight the invader, and it was impossible to preserve any more discipline and regularity among them than their patriotism and the dangers of the moment imposed. Fighting without pay, clothing, or provisions supplied by a government, compelled to care for their families as well as to provide for their own wants, they were likely to go home at planting or harvest time, or simply when the going got too dreary. Therefore, brigade strength fluctuated from as few as 20 or 30 men to as many as several hundred, and Marion had to plan his operations accordingly. He seldom could count on more than 150 to 200 men.

Marion's enemies charged that it was not patriotism but the appeal of plunder that held his men together. But Marion made himself clear on the subject: "Any soldier of any denomination who is found taking any article from any plantation either from white or black will be deemed a marauder & plunderer & shall suffer immediate death."

Despite their irregularities, when Marion came to disband his men in December, 1782, he could say with complete sincerity, "No citizens in the world have ever done more than they have." It was true of them. And it was true of him.

Marion was born in the country he defended to a second-generation French Huguenot family on the Cooper River in South Carolina. As a boy he lived in the vicinity of Georgetown, where he hunted and fished the salt marshes and inland swamps and semitropical woods. When he was 23 and his father, an unsuccessful planter, died, he and his

The dashing Marion was idolized by his troops in much the way the legendary Robin Hood was.

mother and a brother settled for a time in upper St. John's in Berkeley County. The tradition is that he served in a mounted troop on a bootless expedition to the Cherokee country in the first flare-up of the French and Indian War on the Carolina frontier. Two years later, as a light-infantry lieutenant in a 1761 campaign against the Cherokee, he won the praise of his commanding officer as an "active, brave, and hardy soldier; and an excellent partisan officer."

Shortly before the Revolution he acquired a place of his own on the Santee River and was just getting his bachelor house in order when war came. He was elected a captain of the Second South Carolina Continental Regiment, steadily rose in Continental rank, served in the defense of Fort Sullivan in 1776 and the assault on Savannah in 1779, and for a time was in field command of the Southern Army when it wintered near the Georgia border. Through peaceful garrison times and stormy, he shared every fortune of his regiment except its last, when General Benjamin Lincoln surrendered his entire army, including the Second South Carolina, to Sir Henry Clinton at Charleston on May 12, 1780. Marion was not among the nearly 5,500 men who capitulated. For the last several weeks before the

263

fall of the city he had been convalescing at home from an ankle injury.

With Lincoln's surrender, the worst disaster the Americans had suffered in all the war, the American cause both North and South seemed all but lost. In the North, Washington's worn-out army lay deteriorating in New Jersey. The French, upon whom he had relied for reinforcements, were bottled up by a British fleet at Newport. And an enfeebled Congress and an apathetic people were allowing their rebellion to expire from sheer exhaustion. In the South, Georgia had already been occupied by the British since the winter of 1779, and within three weeks after Lincoln's surrender, South Carolina appeared to be totally subjugated. Without firing a shot, British garrisons occupied a chain of posts commanding the interior from Augusta on the Savannah River and Ninety-six on the Carolina frontier, northward to Rocky Mount, Hanging Rock, and Camden, and eastward to Cheraw and Georgetown on the coast.

To the enemy's surprise and consternation, however, the paralysis that at first seized the South Carolinians was short-lived. Lord Charles Cornwallis had hardly reported "everything wearing the face of tranquility and submission" when patriot guerrillas began a fierce, harassing warfare against him.

The partisans took some encouragement from reports that a small, new Continental army had arrived in North Carolina; around this nucleus the militia of Virginia and the Carolinas might build a force strong enough to stop the northward advance of the redcoats. In late July, when his ankle would carry him, Marion rode northward to join it with a little troop of neighbors and former army comrades. According to a Continental officer, they were "distinguished by small black leather caps and the wretchedness of their attire; their number did not exceed 20 men and boys, some white, some black, and all mounted, but most of them miserably equipped." Nevertheless, General Horatio Gates, commanding the army, recognized the value of Marion's familiarity with the country and ordered him and "the Volunteers Horse of So Carolina" to "march with and attend" him as he advanced toward the enemy's key post at Camden.

While on the march, the Marion story has it, Gates received a request from Major John James for an officer to take command of a brigade he had raised among the Scotch-Irish of Williamsburg Township on the Black River. Gates promptly assigned Marion to the command with orders to use the brigade to seize the Santee River crossings behind Camden and cut off British communication with that post and its avenue of retreat to Charleston.

Marion took command of James' brigade on Lynche's Creek about the 10th of August, 1780, and his partisan career began. After two lightning attacks on strong Tory encampments in the neighborhood, he divided his 70 men and sent a party under his old friend, Major Peter Horry, east of Lenud's Ferry on the Santee to destroy all boats and cover the crossings, while he marched westward for Murray's Ferry. After coming down on a British guard there on the night of the 23rd, scattering the redcoats and burning the ferryboats, he turned upriver toward Nelson's Ferry, 25 miles away.

Near dusk he picked up a British deserter who told him that Gates' army, upon reaching Camden, had been routed by the British on the 16th with incredible losses. From the deserter he also learned that a British escort with 150 Continental prisoners from Camden planned to rest that night at a house north of Nelson's Ferry. Without sharing with his men the depressing news of Gates' defeat, for fear they would desert him, he pushed his march all night and descended on the escort at dawn. Trapping many of the redcoats in the house, he killed two, wounded five, took 20 prisoners, and released the captured Continentals. But Marion's men heard from the prisoners that Gates had been defeated, and half of them slipped away within an hour. Marion, discovering that a heavy British patrol was in his rear, sent his prisoners toward North Carolina and retreated eastward toward the Pee Dee to make a junction with Major Horry.

Marion had no idea where the remnant of Gates' army was, or when or if it would ever be in "condition to act again." Colonel Thomas Sumter, who had bedeviled the enemy in the west, had been cut to pieces two days after the Camden debacle. Marion's little brigade was the only rebel force left intact in the state. With most of his men gone home, he now was forced after a couple of brushes with the enemy to withdraw into North Carolina.

Within two weeks, however, he had heard from Gates at Hillsboro: North Carolina was aroused, the army was putting itself back together; in South Carolina, Whig militia was assembling. Unfortunately, the Tories were gathering, too, and Gates would be pleased, he wrote, if Marion would advance to the Little Pee Dee River and disperse them. At the same time Marion heard from South Carolina that north of Georgetown the enemy had laid waste a path 70 miles long and 15 miles wide as a punishment to the inhabitants who had "joined Marion and Horry in their late incursion"; the men who had left him at Nelson's Ferry were spoiling for revenge and ready to come out again. So on a Sunday evening, the 24th of September, with only 30 or 40 men, Marion

marched back into the heart of the enemy's northeasternmost defenses in South Carolina around Kingston.

The marches and actions that ensued between Marion and the British and Tories were shrewdly planned, smoothly executed, and highly damaging to the enemy. Marion brought to them not only the training of an officer of the regular service and the remembered experience of Indian-style fighting on the frontier, but also an intimate knowledge of the country. And it was the terrain that gave the native fighter a distinct advantage. It was unbelievably flat, unbelievably wet, and unbelievably wild. North and south some 80 miles from Charleston and west some 50 were its roughly figured boundaries, and down across it swept seven large rivers and many smaller ones. For miles bordering them were vast swamps. And between the swamps were the forbidding shrub bogs, spongy tangles of impenetrable vegetation. No roads crossed the swamps and bogs, except the secret paths of the hunter. But it was country that Marion

Marion and his roughly dressed men, few of whom had been issued uniforms, cross the Pee Dee River on makeshift rafts, with some of the men swimming the horses by ropes.

265

Major General Nathanael Greene was Marion's commanding officer. Here he is painted by Charles Willson Peale.

Colonel Henry Lee, known as Light Horse Harry, joined Marion against the British. He was also painted by Peale.

knew and understood, so for him its trails became avenues of swift surprise attack and safe retreat, its swamps and bogs his covert.

In this country during that fall of 1780, Marion's men fought at Black Mingo, northwest of Georgetown. It was another night attack, but their horses' hoofs clattering on a wooden bridge gave them away, so they lost the element of surprise and learned ever after to lay down their blankets when crossing a bridge near the enemy. They raided Georgetown, but could not draw the garrison out of the town redoubt for a stand-up fight. Another night they pounced on Tory militia at Tarcote Swamp, near the forks of Black River.

These were small engagements, but as the weeks passed into winter, Lord Cornwallis began to feel the cumulative effect of them. When Marion had retreated into North Carolina in September, Cornwallis had advanced toward Virginia as far north as Charlotte before his detached left wing had been destroyed by rebel frontiersmen at Kings Mountain, and he had

stumbled back 60 miles to Winnsboro to recover himself. In that hamlet, northwest of Camden, Cornwallis encamped for three miserable, wet months, October to January, and his letters from there make it reasonably clear that, although much of his strength had been lost at Kings Mountain and he had to await reinforcements from New York, it was the work of the partisans, especially of Marion, that tied him to Winnsboro and prevented his moving northward again.

The one man Cornwallis thought capable of running down and destroying the elusive Marion was Lieutenant Colonel Banastre Tarleton. In South Carolina, after his savage slaughter of Buford's troops at the Waxhaws, Tarleton was known as The Butcher and was without question the most bitterly hated of all the redcoats. In the British army, where his loyalist legion was famed for its energy, prowess, and daring, he had risen swiftly and at 26 was regarded as perhaps the most valuable leader of mounted troops. "I therefore sent Tarleton," Cornwallis reported, "who pursued Marion for several days, obliged his corps to take to the swamps. . . ."

There was more to it than that: Marion led Tarleton a chase in that November of 1780. Tarleton was 16 miles north of Nelson's Ferry when he discovered that Marion was a few miles south and struck out after him. About dark Marion cut through the Wood-yard, a broad and tangled swamp, and camped for the night six miles beyond it. Tarleton dared not cross the Woodyard in the dark. As he was riding around it in the morning, Marion continued down Black River 35 miles through woods and swamps and bogs, where there was no road. Tarleton, after making his way for seven hours through swamps and defiles, hit 23 miles of fair road and then ran into Ox Swamp, where the chase went out of him.

Tradition has it that when Tarleton turned back (or was called off by a courier with orders to turn about and go after Sumter in the west), he gave Marion his sobriquet: "Come on, my boys, let's go back. As for this damned old fox, the devil himself could not catch him."

For several more weeks the old fox was busily gnawing at British supply trains and posts and parties. Then, with his ammunition and supplies nearly exhausted, he took up an encampment in a romantic spot not far from the original ground of the Williamsburg men. It was called Snow's Island and was a large, high river-swamp plateau at the joining of Lynche's Creek with the Great Pee Dee. Here, deep in a forest of cypress, laurel, and pine, protected by the watercourses and tangles of canebrake and vines, he made a supply depot and rest camp that served him, off and on, for the rest of the war.

Through the rest of the winter of 1780 and into the spring of 1781, Marion played his partisan role while great events wrought great changes in the condition of the American cause in the South. In December, General Nathanael Greene arrived at Char-lotte to succeed Gates in command of the Continental Army of the Southern Depart-ment. By mid-April, 1781, in perhaps the most

Banastre Tarleton, Marion's hated pursuer, was known as The Butcher. By Sir Joshua Reynolds.

brilliant campaign of the war, he had maneuvered a greatly weakened and confused Cornwallis into Virginia and returned to South Carolina to battle for repossession of the state.

As Greene advanced toward Camden, Marion, joined by the splendid legion of young Light Horse Harry Lee, moved against the inner chain of British posts on the Santee and Congaree. Fort Watson, their first objective, was a tremendous stockaded work crowning an ancient Indian mound that rose almost 40 feet above the surrounding plain, north of Nelson's Ferry on the Santee. When Marion and Lee failed after a week to starve out the garrison by siege, they managed to effect a surrender by firing down on the fort from a log tower, devised by a country major of Marion's brigade who probably had never heard of the warring Romans.

By May 6, when they reached Fort Motte on the Congaree, Marion and Lee had a light fieldpiece, begged from Greene's army, but it did them no good. Fort Motte consisted of a strong stockade with outer trenches and an abatis built about a handsome brick mansion on a commanding piece of ground. They spent six days digging parallels and trenches and mounting their gun, but the fieldpiece failed to make a dent in the heavy timbers of the stockade or the walls of the house. Again the attackers resorted to primitive methods. Getting up close under cover of the siege lines, a man of Marion's brigade flung ignited pitch balls on the roof, set it afire, and smoked the enemy out.

One by one the British posts fell. After repulsing Greene, the British evacuated Camden. Augusta surrendered, and Fort Granby. The British blew up their own fort at Nelson's Ferry. Marion dashed to Georgetown and this time took it. Greene himself unsuccessfully laid siege to Ninety-six, but the enemy soon evacuated it and pulled back and consolidated at Orangeburg on the Edisto. Marion, Sumter, and Lee spent a vigorous summer striking behind the enemy army, ranging almost to Charleston, while Greene refreshed his hard-marched army in the oak-and-hickory woods of the High Hills of Santee below Camden.

Late in August, Greene came down from the High Hills to fight his last pitched battle of the war, at Eutaw Springs near Nelson's Ferry, on September 8. For the first time since the assault on Savannah in 1779, Marion found himself in formal battle, in command of the right wing of Greene's front line. The whole first line was made up of North and South Carolina militia. It must have seemed strange to Marion's partisans to be there. But for once the militia did not panic; before falling back under enemy pressure, they delivered 17 rounds and wrung from Greene praise for a firmness that he said "would have graced the veterans of the great King of Prussia."

It was pretty much a drawn battle. Both sides retreated. But Greene had damaged the British so severely that soon they withdrew into their lines at Charleston and never emerged again.

Although patriots and loyalists killed one another with unrelenting bitterness for more than a year longer, the question of ultimate victory in the South was settled. On the day following the battle of Eutaw Springs, a French fleet returned to Chesapeake Bay in Virginia and sealed the fate of Cornwallis, whom Greene had driven into a faraway trap at a village called Yorktown.

In December of the next year, 1782, under the gnarled live oaks at Wadboo plantation, Marion discharged his brigade, its mission accomplished.

After the war, Marion married his cousin and lived out his last years in comfort as a small planter on the Santee. When he died in 1795, it made scarcely a stir; he was simply another old officer of the Revolution. Today many of his battle sites are hidden by towns, roads, and manmade lakes. But the old maps show where he rode and the battle documents tell what he did, and it was a magnificent performance. So perhaps it was justice, after all, that Parson Weems came along.

George F. Scheer is co-author of Rebels and Redcoats *and the editor of* Private Yankee Doodle, *a Revolutionary War soldier's autobiography. He was a general editor of the Meridian Documents of American History series.*

Volume 3
ENCYCLOPEDIC SECTION

The two-page reference guide below lists the entries by categories. The entries in this section supplement the subject matter covered in the text of this volume. A **cross-reference** (*see*) means that a separate entry appears elsewhere in this section. However, certain important persons and events mentioned here have individual entries in the Encyclopedic Section of another volume. Consult the Index in Volume 18.

AMERICAN MILITARY LEADERS

AMERICAN STATESMEN

BRITISH MILITARY LEADERS

John André
Joseph Brant
John Burgoyne
John Butler
Sir Henry Clinton
Charles Cornwallis
Thomas Gage

Sir William Howe
Sir John Johnson
Josiah Martin
Sir Peter Parker
John Pitcairn
Barry St. Leger
Sir Banastre Tarleton

BRITISH STATESMEN

Edmund Burke
Frederick Howard Carlisle
Thomas Fairfax
Charles James Fox
Thomas Gage

George III
Josiah Martin
Frederick North
Charles Rockingham
Second Earl of Shelburne

FRENCH MILITARY LEADERS

Count d'Estaing
Count de Grasse

Louis XVI
Count de Rochambeau

PATRIOT LEADERS AND LEGENDS

Margaret Cochrane Corbin
William Dawes
John Glover
Nathan Hale
Mary Ludwig Hays

Molly Pitcher
Samuel Prescott
Paul Revere
Betsy Ross
Joseph Warren

THE NEW REPUBLIC

Articles of Confederation
Congress of the Confederation
Continental Association
Continental Congress

Declaration of Independence
First Continental Congress
Olive Branch Petition
Second Continental Congress
Treaty of Paris

THE REVOLUTIONARY WAR

Bonhomme Richard
Society of the Cincinnati
Continental Army

Green Mountain Boys
Hessians
Minutemen
Valley Forge

THOUGHT AND CULTURE

Common Sense
John Singleton Copley
Benjamin Franklin
Philip Freneau
Thomas Jefferson

Thomas Paine
primogeniture
The Rights of Man
John Trumbull
Benjamin West
Phillis Wheatley

A

ALLEN, Ethan (1738–1789). The leader of the **Green Mountain Boys** (*see*), Allen waged guerrilla warfare on behalf of Vermont's independence and took part in several important battles within the first six months of the Revolution. He was born in Litchfield, Connecticut, and served briefly in the French and Indian War (1754–1763). Allen and his two brothers settled about 1769 in the territory of Vermont, which was then known as the New Hampshire Grants. The ownership of this area was being contested by New Hampshire and New York. Allen took sides with New Hampshire and organized the Green Mountain Boys in 1770 to drive out the "Yorkers." The guerrilla activities of this backwoods militia so frustrated New York's Governor William Tryon (1725–1788) that in 1774 he offered a reward for Allen's arrest. When the Revolution started the following year, Allen, together with **Benedict Arnold** (*see*), seized Fort Ticonderoga. Allen and the Green Mountain Boys subsequently wrested control of Lake Champlain from the British. In the fall of 1775, he rashly tried to capture Montreal and was taken prisoner. Soon after his release in 1778, Allen was made a major general of the Vermont militia, but he devoted himself more to fighting New Yorkers on the Vermont border than to fighting the British. He petitioned Congress to recognize Vermont's claim to statehood, but his request was denied. Allen entered into negotiations with the English in 1780 to make Vermont a British province in return for protection against New York. It has never been determined whether he did this for selfish motives—Allen and his brothers claimed 300,000 acres of Vermont land—or as a ruse to force Congress to give in to his demands for statehood. However, with the signing of the Treaty of Paris in 1783, the plan was dropped. Allen died in Burlington in 1789, two years before Vermont became a state.

ANDRÉ, John (1751?–1780). André represented **Sir Henry Clinton** (*see*), the British commander in North America, in negotiating with **Benedict Arnold** (*see*) for the betrayal of West Point in 1780. He was captured by militiamen behind American lines, tried, and hanged as a spy. André had rejected a career in his father's London business to obtain a lieutenant's commission in the British army in 1771. Sent to Canada three years later, he was captured during the American siege of Quebec in 1775 but freed the following year. General Clinton made him adjutant general of the army in 1779 and placed him in charge of intelligence operations.

When Arnold offered to betray West Point, André, who knew the fort commander's wife, Margaret, was assigned to negotiate with him. The two met secretly at night on September 21, 1780, on the banks of the Hudson. Arnold handed over the plans to the fortress at West Point, the key post in the defense of the Hudson River Valley. During the meeting, the *Vulcan,* the ship that had brought André to the meeting, was fired on and had to retreat downstream. Forced to return on horseback, André changed from his uniform into civilian clothes. He was stopped and taken prisoner by American troops, who found the plans to West Point in his boots. When Arnold learned of André's capture, he fled behind British lines. The André case is famous in military legal history. Because André had disguised himself in civilian clothes, he was considered a spy rather than a prisoner of war. He was court-martialed on September 29, 1780, and sentenced to die. Despite British demands, George Washington refused to set aside the verdict. André was executed October 2, 1780, at Tappan, New York.

André sketched this portrait of himself the day before he was hanged.

ARNOLD, Benedict (1741–1801). Benedict Arnold was one of America's ablest generals in the Revolution, but his name has become synonymous with the word traitor. Angered because he was ignored for promotion several times, he gave the British valuable military information in return for money and a position in the British army. Arnold was born in Norwich, Connecticut, and ran away from home at 14 to fight in the French and Indian War (1754–1763). After brief service, he deserted and later went to New Haven, where he became a bookseller and druggist and an investor in the West India trade. He subsequently became a captain in the Connecticut militia. After the Battle of Lexington in 1775, he led a company of volunteers to Cambridge, where he was commissioned a colonel by the Massachusetts Committee of Safety. He joined **Ethan Allen** (*see*) of Vermont in the successful assault on Fort Ticonderoga in May, 1775. Arnold then captured a fort on the northern end of Lake Champlain. Despite these victories, the Massachusetts authorities relieved Arnold of his command. **George Washington** (*see*) subsequently appointed him to lead an expedition through Maine to attack Quebec. After a difficult journey through the wilderness, Arnold's force joined an army led by **Richard Montgomery** (*see*), who had come by way of Lakes Champlain and George. Together they unsuccessfully attacked Quebec on December 31, 1775. Montgomery was killed, and Arnold was wounded. Arnold blockaded Quebec until spring and then retreated to Montreal. His brilliant conduct of the contest for control of Lakes Champlain and George in 1776 helped to block the British plan to cut off New England from the other colonies. Nevertheless, the Second Continental Congress (*see* **Continental**

This two-faced effigy of traitor Benedict Arnold was burned in 1780.

Congress) promoted other officers ahead of him, increasing his resentment. Under **Philip Schuyler** and **Horatio Gates** (*see both*), Arnold fought gallantly. In the midst of the Saratoga campaign against **John Burgoyne** (*see*), Arnold quarreled with Gates and was relieved of his command. However, he stayed with the troops and was seriously wounded. Congress thanked Arnold for this service, and Washington placed him in command of Philadelphia in 1778. There he ran into trouble with Pennsylvania officials, who were jealous of his authority. They accused him of misconduct. While awaiting court-martial, Arnold, further embittered and now heavily in debt, secretly wrote the British commander in New York, **Sir Henry Clinton** (*see*), about joining the British side. Under the instructions of the court-martial, Washington reprimanded him. Nevertheless, Arnold obtained the command of West Point in the summer of 1780. Still embittered, he met secretly on September 21

with **John André** (*see*), Clinton's adjutant general, and handed him the plans for the fort. André was captured two days later, and Arnold was forced to flee to the British lines. The British commissioned him a brigadier general and paid him a substantial sum of money for deserting, but much less than he had hoped for. Arnold subsequently led British raids on Richmond, Virginia, in 1780 and on New London, Connecticut, in 1781. After the British defeat at Yorktown in 1781, Arnold went to England, where he was scorned as a traitor. His subsequent business ventures in the West Indies and Canada failed. Broken in spirit, health, and fortune, Arnold died in London on June 14, 1801.

ARTICLES OF CONFEDERATION. The Articles of Confederation—by which the United States was governed from March 1, 1781, to March 4, 1789—preserved the union of American states in the earliest dissent-filled years of the Republic. The Articles represented an attempt to reconcile the need for central control with the unwillingness of the states to submit to a federal governing body. In June, 1776, the Second Continental Congress appointed a committee led by **John Dickinson** (*see*) to write the Articles of Confederation. The committee presented its draft in July. The resulting debate centered upon how the states would be taxed by and represented in the federal government. The Articles also gave Congress the power to fix western boundaries and regulate Indian affairs. After some revisions, Congress approved the Articles, and the states ratified them. They became effective on March 1, 1781, when a new governing body, the Congress of the Confederation, took over running the Republic. The Congress of the Confederation was dependent on the states to raise funds, enlist troops, and regulate commerce. A movement in favor of a stronger government led to a tariff convention in 1786 at Annapolis, Maryland. Although attendance was poor and the meeting did not accomplish much, a resolution was adopted at the suggestion of Alexander Hamilton (1755–1804) of New York to hold a constitutional convention the following year in Philadelphia. The Constitutional Convention met at Independence Hall on May 14, 1787. It drew up the United States Constitution, which officially replaced the Articles of Confederation on March 4, 1789.

B

BARRY, John (1745–1803). Barry was commander of the first regularly commissioned American ship to capture a British warship in the Revolutionary War. Born in Ireland, Barry settled in Philadelphia about 1760, where he became a prosperous merchant-ship captain and owner. An early champion of the patriot cause, Barry volunteered his services to the Second Continental Congress at the outbreak of the war and was given command of the brig *Lexington*. On April 17, 1776, he seized the British tender *Edward*. Considered second only in daring and skill to **John Paul Jones** (*see*), Barry subsequently commanded several other warships during the Revolution and captured many important prizes. In March, 1783, as captain of the *Alliance*, he fought the last naval engagement of the war, in which he defeated, but was unable to capture, the British ship *Sybil*. Barry was appointed the first commodore of the newly established United States Navy in 1794. Between 1798 and 1801, he served two terms as commander of American naval forces in the West Indies.

BONHOMME RICHARD. The *Bonhomme Richard* was the flagship of **John Paul Jones** (*see*) during his successful engagement with the *Serapis* off the coast of England on September 23, 1779. Originally named the *Duras,* she was an old, unseaworthy French merchant ship that **Louis XVI** (*see*) had given to the American government that year. Jones refitted the ship with 40 guns and renamed her the *Bonhomme Richard* in honor of **Benjamin Franklin** (*see*), whose *Poor Richard's Almanack* was then popular reading in France. Jones captured the *Serapis* after a three-and-a-half-hour battle, although the *Bonhomme Richard,* badly damaged in the fight, finally sank.

BOWDOIN, James (1726–1790). The political career of Bowdoin, one of the wealthiest men in New England, spanned the Revolution. A Harvard graduate and heir to a large fortune, he was first elected a member of the Massachusetts General Court in 1753. He also served (1757–1774) on the council that advised the governor. Bowdoin's influence helped to keep the council united and aligned with colonial interests. Among his associates were Samuel Adams (1722–1803) and **John Hancock** (*see*). Bowdoin opposed British trade restrictions and wrote many protests and petitions to the British that emphasized the economic side of the dispute. In 1777, he was elected to the Second Continental Congress but was unable to serve because of poor health, and Hancock took his place. In 1779, Bowdoin was elected president of the convention charged with drawing up the Massachusetts constitution (*see p. 247*). Six years later, Bowdoin was elected governor and suppressed Shays' Rebellion (1786–1787), an armed uprising of discontented farmers. He was also active in 1788 in getting Massachusetts to ratify the United States Constitu-

John Barry

tion. In addition to his political career, Bowdoin, a physics and astronomy enthusiast, was the founder and first president of the American Academy of Arts and Sciences. Bowdoin College in Maine was founded in 1794 with an endowment provided in his will.

BRANT, Joseph (1742–1807). Brant, a Mohawk chief whose Indian name was Thayendanegea, helped obtain Indian support for the British cause during the Revolutionary War. At the age of 13, he fought with the British in the French and Indian War (1754–1763). He entered Moor's Indian Charity School in Lebanon, Connecticut, in 1761 and became a Christian. In 1763, he fought with the Iroquois, who sided with the British during Pontiac's Rebellion (1763–1766). At the outbreak of the Revolution, Brant visited England, where he was presented at court. On his return to America, he led Indian troops in raids on American settlers. Because of the brutality with which his Indians massacred colonials—notably at the Battle of Oriskany, New York, on August 6, 1777 (*see* **Nicholas Herkimer**), and at Cherry Valley, New York, on November 11, 1778—he was known as Monster Brant. After the Revolution, Brant, having failed to negotiate an Indian land settlement with the American government, obtained a Canadian land grant for his Indians in the vicinity of what is now Brantford, Ontario, which was named after him. He devoted his last years to the welfare of his tribe and translated parts of the Bible and the Book of Common Prayer into the Mohawk dialect.

BURGOYNE, John (1722–1792). Burgoyne's surrender of his army to the American forces at Sara-

John Burgoyne

toga (*see pp. 216–220*) in 1777 was the turning point of the Revolutionary War. As a result, France entered the war on the American side. Gentleman Johnny, as he was called, joined the British army at an early age. He served in Portugal during the Seven Years War (1756–1763) and was promoted to brigadier general. In 1775, he was sent to Boston with reinforcements for **Thomas Gage** (*see*). The following year, Burgoyne was made commander of an army and ordered to invade the colonies from Canada by advancing down the Hudson River Valley. He was told that **Sir William Howe** (*see*) would move an army north up the Hudson from New York to join him. The plan was to separate New England from the other colonies. Burgoyne moved south at the end of June, 1777, with about 7,000 British and German troops and several hundred Canadian and Indian scouts. He recaptured Fort Ticonderoga on July 6 and advanced slowly southward until he met an American army commanded by **Horatio Gates** (*see*). Decisively defeated, Burgoyne retreated to Saratoga, where his army, reduced to about 3,500 able-bodied men, was soon surrounded by American forces num-

bering over 17,000. Burgoyne held out in Saratoga, hoping to be relieved by **Sir Henry Clinton** (*see*), but Clinton got no farther than West Point. Cut off and facing hopeless odds, Burgoyne surrendered his army to Gates on October 17, 1777. He returned to England in disgrace and retired from public life. Burgoyne devoted the rest of his time to writing plays. He died on June 4, 1792.

BURKE, Edmund (1729–1797). Considered one of England's greatest political philosophers and orators, Burke was a leading spokesman for the rights of American colonists in Parliament. A native of Ireland, Burke entered Parliament in 1765 and soon became an outspoken critic of the colonial policies of **George III** (*see*). In 1774, he urged repeal of the tea tax, warning Parliament not to make American colonists the "pack-horses of every tax you choose to impose, without the least share in granting them." The tax, he said, "yields no revenue;

Edmund Burke

it yields nothing but discontent, disorder, disobedience. . . ." The following year, in his speech "Conciliation with America," Burke again urged a more liberal policy toward the colonists. After the Revolution began, he condemned the use of Indians in fighting the Americans. Before his retirement from Parliament in 1794, Burke supported efforts to abolish the slave trade. Although a champion of many liberal reforms, Burke was a conservative in matters of political change. His condemnation of the French Revolution in 1790 prompted **Thomas Paine** to write *The Rights of Man* (*see both*).

BUTLER, John (1728–1794?). Butler, a pro-British resident of New York's Mohawk Valley, commanded the Indians used by **Barry St. Leger** (*see*) in his unsuccessful attack on Fort Stanwix at Rome, New York, in 1777. Butler formed a combined battalion of Indians and settlers the following year for the invasion of the Wyoming Valley in Pennsylvania, an expedition that became notorious for the Indian atrocities committed against the residents of the area. Butler and his Mohawk ally, **Joseph Brant** (*see*), were finally defeated at the Battle of Newtown, near present-day Elmira, New York, on August 29, 1779, by the American general **John Sullivan** (*see*). After the war, he was appointed an Indian commissioner by the British for the Niagara district of Canada.

C

CARLISLE, Frederick Howard (1748–1825). Lord Carlisle was head of a British delegation sent to America by **Frederick North** (*see*) in 1778 to offer peace terms to the rebelling colonies. The mission

was inspired by the British defeat at Saratoga on October 17, 1777. Britain, hoping to make peace before France could enter the war, was willing to allow the colonies to govern themselves, provided they remained part of the British Empire. However, the Second Continental Congress refused to negotiate with Carlisle and signed an alliance with France instead. Among other public offices he later held, Carlisle was viceroy of Ireland from 1780 to 1782.

CINCINNATI, Society of the. Established in May, 1783, by the officers of the Continental Army, the Society of the Cincinnati was the first veterans' group in the United States. It was named after Lucius Quinctius Cincinnatus, a Roman military leader of the fifth century B.C., who returned to his farm and family after victory rather than accept a position in the government. The society was largely the idea of the American general **Henry Knox** (*see*), who wrote its charter. George Washington was its first president. The society's aims were to preserve the ideals of the Revolution, to maintain the friendships formed by the participating officers, and to provide financial aid to needy members. Only officers were eligible for membership. When a charter member died, membership passed to his eldest son or to another male relative whom the society considered suitable. Because of its exclusive nature, the society was severely criticized in the beginning as being a military aristocracy. By the 1790s, however, the outcry against the Cincinnati had died down, and the group is still active today.

CLINTON, Sir Henry (1738?–1795). Clinton was born in New-

foundland, where his father, George Clinton (1686?–1761), was governor. After his father was appointed governor of New York, Clinton served in the New York militia and later fought in Germany during the Seven Years War (1756–1763). He returned to America as a general in 1775 and fought in the Battle of Bunker Hill. In 1777, he was knighted for his part the previous year in the Battle of Long Island. Clinton replaced **Sir William Howe** (*see*) as commander in chief in North America in 1778. He immediately withdrew his forces from Philadelphia to New York, successfully repulsing attacks led by **George Washington** and **Charles Lee** (*see both*) at Monmouth. Clinton invaded South Carolina in 1779 and seized Charleston on May 12, 1780. He returned to New York, where, fearing an attack by Washington in 1781, he refused to send troops to **Charles Cornwallis** (*see*) at Yorktown. When he finally did dispatch a relief force, it arrived too late. In 1794, Clinton was appointed governor of Gibraltar. He died there on December 23, 1795.

COMMON SENSE. This pamphlet, written by **Thomas Paine** (*see*), played an important role in convincing many American colonists to support independence from England. It was published in Philadelphia on January 10, 1776, and more than 100,000 copies were sold in three months. The pamphlet attacked the British monarchy and described the economic advantages to be gained by separation from Great Britain. *Common Sense* also helped to bolster the morale of the soldiers in the American army. George Washington reported that the pamphlet was "working a powerful change . . . in the minds of many men." Some historians consider *Common Sense* the most influential writing of its kind ever published.

CONGRESS OF THE CONFEDERATION. *See* **Continental Congress.**

CONTINENTAL ARMY. Created by the Second Continental Congress in June, 1775, the Continental Army was commanded by **George Washington** (*see*). It was paid by Congress, which had trouble obtaining the funds from the colonies. Soldiers and officers were recruited from the already existing militia regiments of the individual colonies and from abroad as well. In contrast with militiamen, who could enlist for short periods, the soldiers of the Continental Army, when it was first formed, had to enlist for a year. After 1777, the term of enlistment was extended to three years or the duration of the war. Many men were reluctant to commit themselves for such a long time. Most of the soldiers were poorly trained. Only after the spring of 1778, after being trained by **Baron Friedrich von Steuben** at **Valley Forge** (*see both*), were the Continental regulars an equal match for the well-disciplined British soldiers. The army was split by sectional differences. It also suffered from lack of weapons, food, clothing, and medical supplies. Few Continentals had uniforms, and at times many even went without shoes. Some of these hardships were due to the difficulties of transportation, discord between the colonies, and mismanagement. The currency issued by Congress was virtually worthless, and merchants and farmers often refused to accept it in exchange for goods. The soldiers at Valley Forge who chanted "no pay, no clothes, no provisions, no rum" aptly described the stark realities of their existence. Although it is impossible to determine the exact number of men who served in the Continental Army during the Revolution, most estimates place the figure at about 230,000. In addition, about 164,000 men served in the militia. The number of soldiers serving at any one time fluctuated widely, and desertions were common. The fact that the army did not disintegrate completely is a testimony to General Washington's leadership.

CONTINENTAL ASSOCIATION. This association was formed by the First Continental Congress in the autumn of 1774 to organize a boycott of British goods. The association was unusual because, unlike previous attempts at boycotting, its members agreed to ban American exports to England as well as English imports to America. In addition, the Continental Association set up local committees to punish violators of the boycott by publicizing their names. By April, 1775, the association was active in 12 colonies. The colonists hoped the boycott would force Great Britain to relax its trade restrictions. However, the attempt failed because the British found other outlets to replace their American market. Thus, there was no reason for British merchants to pressure Parliament to change its restrictive colonial policies. The Continental Association represented one of the last peaceful attempts to settle the growing differences between the American colonies and the mother country.

CONTINENTAL CONGRESS. There were two Continental Congresses, each with a different purpose. The First Continental Congress, which convened in 1774 at the urging of Virginia, was made up of delegates from 12 colonies who joined together to try to restore harmony with England over colonial rights. Only Georgia was not represented. The Congress met in Philadelphia from September 5 to October 26. Its major accomplishments were (1) a declaration to **George III** (*see*) listing colonial rights and grievances; (2) the organization of the **Continental Association** (*see*) to boycott trade with Britain; and (3) a resolution calling for another Congress to meet again in Philadelphia on May 10, 1775, if the grievances had not been removed. By the time the Second Continental Congress convened, the Revolution was already three weeks old. This Congress served as the unofficial central government of all 13 colonies for the next six years. Massachusetts offered its colonial forces, which were then besieging the British at Boston, as the basis of the **Continental Army** (*see*). The Congress accepted and on June 15 appointed **George Washington** (*see*) as the commander in chief. On July 2, 1776, Congress approved the resolution of **Richard Henry Lee** (*see*) to separate the colonies from England, and two days later it adopted the **Declaration of Independence** (*see*), the formal announcement of that separation. The Second Continental Congress was then succeeded on March 1, 1781, by the Congress of the Confederation, which became the official governing body of the new republic under the **Articles of Confederation** (*see*). These Articles, which had been adopted to provide a permanent form of government, proved inefficient in practice. As a result, a new framework for government, the Constitution, was adopted and put into effect on March 4, 1789, when the United States Congress assembled as a legislative body. The current Congresses date from that time.

CONWAY, Thomas (1735?–1800). Conway, a brigadier general in the Continental Army, played a prominent role in an alleged plot to replace George Washington as commander in chief in 1777. An Irish soldier of fortune, Conway had served in the French army (1749–1776) before accepting a commission in America in 1777. He fought under Washington at Brandywine and Germantown. Washington subsequently tried to block Conway's promotion, but the Second Continental Congress overruled him and made Conway a major general and the inspector general of the army. Resenting Washington's refusal to promote him, Conway severely criticized the commander in chief in a letter to **Horatio Gates** (*see*). His remarks were made public, probably by **James Wilkinson** (*see*), a member of Gates' staff. Together

John Singleton Copley

with criticism of Washington by certain members of Congress, Conway's letter started the rumor that a plot, known as Conway's Cabal, was being formed to remove Washington from command and replace him with Gates. In 1778, Conway resigned his commission. On July 4 of that same year, he was wounded in a duel with another officer over some critical remarks he made about Washington. Conway subsequently returned to Europe and rejoined the French army. In 1787, he was made governor-general of French possessions in India.

COPLEY, John Singleton (1738–1815). Together with Gilbert Stuart (1755–1828) and **John Trumbull** (*see*), Copley was one of early America's greatest painters. He was a professional portrait painter by the age of 18, after apparently being trained by his stepfather, Peter Pelham (1695–1751), a painter and engraver. During the 1760s and early 1770s, Copley painted many of Boston's foremost citizens—including Paul Revere (*see p. 187*) and Samuel Adams (*see p. 246*). Copley's reputation was established when his "Boy with the Squirrel" was exhibited in London in 1766 through the help of **Benjamin West** (*see*). In 1769, he married the daughter of a wealthy pro-British tea merchant, who was later entrusted with the shipment that led to the Boston Tea Party on December 16, 1773. Copley left Boston for a tour of Europe in 1774 and settled in England the following year. There he painted many celebrated persons, including the royal family. He was elected a member of the Royal Academy in 1783. Copley intended to return to the United States but suffered two paralytic strokes and died on

September 9, 1815. His son, John Singleton Copley (1772–1863), later Baron Lyndhurst, served three times as lord chancellor of England.

CORBIN, Margaret Cochrane. *See* **Molly Pitcher.**

Charles Cornwallis

CORNWALLIS, Charles (1738–1805). The surrender of the British army at Yorktown by Lord Cornwallis in 1781 marked the end of the American Revolution. Cornwallis joined the British army in 1756 and served in Germany during the Seven Years War (1756–1763). He became a member of Parliament in 1760 and spoke out against taxing the American colonies. However, when the Revolution started in 1775, Cornwallis volunteered for service and was sent to America. He served under **Sir William Howe** (*see*) at the Battle of Long Island in 1776 and at Brandywine in 1777. In 1778, Cornwallis was appointed second in command of the British army under **Sir Henry Clinton** (*see*). He sailed with Clinton from New York to South Carolina in 1780. They captured Charleston on May 12. Three months later, Cornwallis defeated **Horatio Gates** (*see*) at Camden. In March, 1781, he defeated Gates' successor, **Nathanael Greene** (*see*), at the Battle of Guilford Court House, but he sustained heavy losses. Cornwallis retreated to Wilmington, North Carolina, and then moved north into Virginia. He urged Clinton to abandon New York so that they could concentrate their forces in Virginia, but Clinton refused. After several inconclusive skirmishes in July, 1781, against forces under the command of the **Marquis de Lafayette** (*see*), Cornwallis withdrew to Yorktown, where he was subsequently hemmed in by combined American and French land and naval forces. He surrendered his army on October 19, and the military phase of the Revolution was ended. The following year, Cornwallis was sent back to Britain in exchange for **Henry Laurens** (*see*), a captured American diplomat. Cornwallis was later appointed governor-general of India (1786–1793) and viceroy of Ireland (1798–1801). He was again appointed governor-general of India in 1805 but died shortly after his arrival there.

D

DAWES, William (1745–1799). Dawes was chosen, along with **Paul Revere** (*see*), to spread the alarm if British troops stationed

William Dawes

in Boston should attempt to raid the surrounding towns. Dawes was a tanner by trade and was active in the revolutionary movement. On the night of April 18, 1775, the British general **Thomas Gage** (*see*) sent out a detachment of soldiers to destroy military supplies at Concord and to arrest Samuel Adams (1722–1803) and **John Hancock** (*see*). The two rebel leaders were hiding out at a parsonage in Lexington, about 10 miles away. Revere set off on horseback from the mainland side of the Charles River when he saw a signal light in the North Church tower. In Boston, **Joseph Warren** (*see*) summoned Dawes and sent him by way of Brighton Bridge and the Cambridge Road. Slipping through the British lines, Dawes, also on horseback, met Revere in Lexington, and together they warned Hancock and Adams. Then, joined by **Samuel Prescott** (*see*), who was visiting in Lexington, they headed for Concord, about 10 miles farther on, rousing the inhabitants along the way. Revere was stopped by a British patrol, but either Prescott or Dawes reached Concord and gave the alarm. Dawes subsequently enlisted in the Continental Army and probably fought at the Battle of Bunker Hill in June, 1775. After the Revolution, he became a grocer in Boston.

DEANE, Silas (1737–1789). Deane, a rich Connecticut lawyer, was America's first diplomat but ended his career in disgrace. An early supporter of anti-British resistance, he was selected in 1769 to be chairman of a committee to boycott British goods. Four years later, he became secretary to the Connecticut Committee of Correspondence, which sent him as a delegate to both Continental Con-

Silas Deane

gresses. In March, 1776, Deane was chosen to seek military and trade assistance in France. He arranged the sending of eight shiploads of military supplies to the colonies in time to support the American victory at Saratoga in the fall of 1777. Deane also helped to enlist a number of European soldiers to aid the American cause —among them such valuable military leaders as **Johann Kalb,** the **Marquis de Lafayette, Casimir Pulaski,** and **Baron von Steuben** (*see all*). In September, 1776, Congress, encouraged by Deane's success, added **Benjamin Franklin** (*see*) and Arthur Lee (1740–1792) to its diplomatic commission in Paris. Through their combined efforts, a military alliance with France was signed in 1778. Deane was ordered home that year to answer charges made by Lee that he was pocketing money intended to pay for French arms. Deane's defense was that he had not been able to keep proper accounts. When he could not disprove the charges, Deane returned to Europe in 1780 in an unsuccessful effort to obtain evidence of his innocence. In 1781, embittered and almost penniless, Deane wrote to friends in the colonies advising them to abandon the Revolution. These letters, which were intercepted by the British and printed in New York, branded Deane as a traitor. He spent the rest of his life in exile.

DECLARATION OF INDEPENDENCE.

The Declaration of Independence, which was adopted on July 4, 1776, contained two main parts. The first, the preamble, stated that man possessed God-given rights of "Life, Liberty and the pursuit of Happiness" (*see pp. 202-203*). The second part contained a list of grievances that concluded by declaring the separation of the American colonies from Great Britain. The Second Continental Congress first debated independence on June 7, 1776, when **Richard Henry Lee** (*see*) proposed that the "connection between them & the state of Great Britain is, & ought to be, totally dissolved." On June 11, Congress, still debating the issue of independence, chose a committee to prepare a formal declaration of separation. It was composed of **Thomas Jefferson, Benjamin Franklin, Robert Livingston, Roger Sherman** (*see all*), and John Adams (1735-1826). Jefferson, picked by the committee to write the document, composed his draft between June 11 and June 28. He borrowed heavily from the English philosopher John Locke (1632-1704), paraphrasing Locke's assertion that man's natural rights included life, liberty, and property. Jefferson differed from Locke in that he ranked the pursuit of happiness as a more important goal than the guarantee of property rights. He gave the document to Adams and Franklin, both of whom made minor changes. On June 28, Jefferson submitted the Declaration to Congress. On July 2, Congress adopted Lee's resolution, which officially separated the "United Colonies" from Britain. Congress then took up the subject of the Declaration. The most important change made by the delegates was to delete a condemnation of the slave trade, a deletion that Jefferson, a slaveholder himself, opposed. The condemnation was defeated by a coalition of Southern slave owners and Northern merchants who operated slave ships. Congress adopted the revised version on July 4. Four days later, the Declaration was read from the balcony of Independence Hall in Philadelphia. To protect the signers from British retaliation, their names were not made public until January 18, 1777. The document is now enshrined in the Library of Congress.

DE GRASSE, Count François Joseph Paul

(1722-1788). De Grasse, a French admiral, helped make possible the American victory at Yorktown in 1781 by repelling a British fleet and preventing any reinforcements from reaching **Charles Cornwallis** (*see*) by sea. De Grasse was sent to America in command of a squadron shortly after France entered the war in 1778. He fought the British in the West Indies, capturing Tobago early in 1781. That summer, de Grasse, at George Washington's request, sailed with his entire force of 28 warships and several troop transports for Yorktown. Cornwallis, meanwhile, had entrenched his forces there and was waiting for a British fleet to

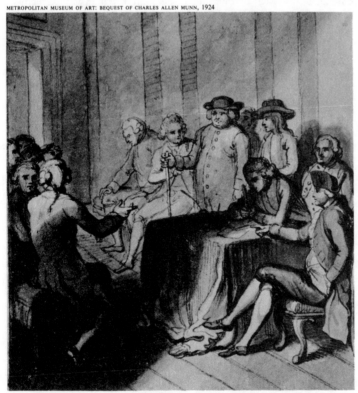

This 1776 sketch shows the signers of the Declaration of Independence.

bring him supplies and reinforcements. De Grasse arrived first. On August 31, he landed 3,000 reinforcements for the **Marquis de Lafayette** (*see*). When the British fleet of 19 ships arrived five days later, de Grasse put to sea and fought an action in which a number of the British vessels were badly damaged. The French admiral then blockaded the entrance to Chesapeake Bay. Cornwallis, under heavy assault and cut off from all aid, surrendered on October 19. De Grasse later returned to the West Indies, where his squadron was defeated by a British fleet under George Rodney (1719–1792) at the Battle of the Saintes on April 12, 1782. After his release, de Grasse was found innocent of negligence by a court-martial. He died in Paris six years later.

DICKINSON, John (1732–1808). Dickinson was one of the few members of the Second Continental Congress who took up arms once independence had been declared in 1776. A lawyer from Philadelphia, Dickinson attended the Stamp Act Congress in 1765, where he opposed resistance to the crown, although he believed that Britain's colonial policies were wrong. After the Battle of Bunker Hill in 1775, Dickinson authored the **Olive Branch Petition** (*see*), which Congress sent to **George III** (*see*) in a futile effort to prevent further bloodshed. Dickinson voted against the Declaration of Independence but enlisted in and served briefly as an officer with the Continental Army that same year. After being defeated for reelection to the Congress, he left the army and returned to an estate he had in Delaware. When the British threatened Philadelphia in 1777, he

served temporarily as a private at the Battle of Brandywine. In 1781, Dickinson was elected president of the Supreme Executive Council of Delaware. Six years later, he represented Delaware at the convention that drafted the United States Constitution, and he personally advocated its ratification.

E

ESTAING, Count Charles Hector d' (1729–1794). Estaing was the French admiral who commanded a fleet sent to aid America against Britain in 1778. Together with American leaders, he planned a combined sea and land attack on British-held Newport, Rhode Island. However, before the attack took place, Estaing decided to fight an English fleet. A storm damaged his vessels, and he sailed to Boston for repairs. Estaing subsequently captured St. Vincent and Grenada in the West Indies. In the summer of 1779, he attacked Savannah but suffered heavy losses and returned to France the following year. After the French Revolution broke out in 1789, Estaing served as com-

Count Charles Hector d'Estaing

mandant of the National Guard and later as an admiral. He testified on behalf of the queen, Marie Antoinette (1755–1793), at her trial in 1793 and the next year followed her to the guillotine.

F

FAIRFAX, Thomas (1693–1781). Fairfax, an English baron, inherited 5,000,000 acres in northern Virginia, between the Rappahannock and Potomac Rivers, from his grandfather, Thomas Culpeper (1635–1689), a former colonial governor of Virginia. Because the colonial authorities disputed his boundaries, he came over from England in 1735 and stayed for two years in order to have his lands surveyed. In 1747, he settled in Virginia. Before he built his mansion, Greenway Court, he lived for a few years with a cousin, Sir William Fairfax, who was the patron of the young George Washington. In 1748, Thomas Fairfax hired Washington as a surveyor to remap his lands. Although he was loyal to the crown and was the only English nobleman living in the colonies at the time of the Revolution, Fairfax went unharmed. However, in 1785, four years after his death, his lands were confiscated by the state of Virginia.

FIRST CONTINENTAL CONGRESS. *See* **Continental Congress.**

FOX, Charles James (1749–1806). Fox, a gifted British orator and champion of people's rights, spent most of his career opposing the policies of **George III** (*see*). He became a member of Parliament in 1768 and joined the administration of **Frederick North** (*see*) as a junior admiralty lord in 1770. He

Charles James Fox

was dismissed in 1774 because of a disagreement with Lord North and the king. During the American Revolution, Fox attacked North's conduct of the war. However, Fox joined North as foreign minister in a coalition government in 1783. The coalition was soon forced out of office by the king, who succeeded in keeping Fox out of power for the next 23 years. Fox continued to advocate reforms in Parliament, along with the abolition of the slave trade. In 1806, Fox became foreign minister again, but died within a few months. His bill abolishing the slave trade became law the following year.

FRANKLIN, Benjamin (1706–1790). Franklin's achievements as a statesman, a writer, a scientist, and an inventor made him the most famous and respected American at the time of the Revolution. One of the ablest diplomats in the history of America, he represented the interests of the colonies in Britain until the eve of the Revolution and served in France during most of the war. He helped negotiate the **Treaty of Paris** (*see*), which formally ended hostilities

on September 3, 1783. Franklin was born in Boston, the son of a soapmaker. He received little formal schooling and was apprenticed to his father at the age of 10. Two years later, he began work in the printing business of his half brother James (1697–1735). Noted for his thrift and hard work, Franklin became a skilled printer and published his own essays under the pen name of Silence Dogood. He moved to Philadelphia in 1723 and by 1730 was publishing the *Pennsylvania Gazette.* From 1732 to 1757, he issued *Poor Richard's Almanack,* a colonial best seller. Many of the homespun sayings ("The cat in gloves catches no mice") and pungent witticisms ("God helps them that help themselves") of Poor Richard have become American proverbs. Among Franklin's extensive writings are his *Autobiography,* which was written between 1771 and 1789, and many political satires. Studying on his own, Franklin mastered French, Italian, Spanish, and Latin. Among his many inventions were the Franklin stove, bifocal glasses, and the lightning rod. His experiments with electricity earned him worldwide renown as a scientist. One of the leading economic thinkers of his day, he advocated the use of paper currency. Franklin pioneered in the organization of circulating libraries, city hospitals, fire companies, and police forces. He also promoted the paving and lighting of streets. In 1727, he organized a debating club that became the American Philosophical Society. In 1751, he started an academy that later developed into the University of Pennsylvania. Franklin's political contributions are equally numerous and impressive. He improved the postal system as a mail official (1753–1774)

for the colonies and was postmaster general (1775–1776) at the outset of the Revolution. Representing Pennsylvania at the Albany Congress in 1754, he drew up a plan of union that laid the groundwork for later efforts to unite the colonies. As an agent for the Pennsylvania Assembly in Britain for almost 20 years before the Revolution, Franklin helped to bring about the repeal of the Stamp Act, which he termed "the mother of mischief." Upon returning to Pennsylvania in 1775, he became a member of the Second Continental Congress, and the next year he worked on a draft of the **Declaration of Independence** (*see*). "We must all hang together," he said after signing this document, "or assuredly we shall all hang separately." He represented America in France from 1777 to 1785, helping to secure loans totaling $60,000,000 to finance the Revolution. After the war, Franklin was chosen president of the Pennsylvania Executive Council and worked to secure ratification of the United States Constitution. His last public act

was to urge Congress to abolish slavery. His death, on April 17, 1790, was mourned throughout the world. Twenty thousand persons attended his funeral. His international fame had been summed up five years before by **Thomas Jefferson** (*see*). Assigned to replace Franklin in France in 1785, Jefferson announced, "No one can replace him, sir; I am only his successor."

FRENEAU, Philip Morin (1752–1832). Freneau is known as the Poet of the American Revolution. He began writing patriotic verse as a student at the College of New Jersey (now Princeton). His poem "The Rising Glory of America" was read at his class commencement in 1771 and published as a pamphlet the next year. When the Revolution started in 1775, Freneau became a revolutionary pamphleteer. A year later, he went to sea. He was captured during a voyage in 1780 and kept aboard the infamous prison ship *Scorpion* in New York Harbor. Upon his release, Freneau published *The British Prison-Ship* (1781), in which he described the terrible treatment of American prisoners of war. During the next three years, Freneau contributed poetry and articles to the Philadelphia *Freeman's Journal*. In 1791, he began publishing the *National Gazette*. Freneau was a staunch supporter of **Thomas Jefferson** (*see*). His journalistic attacks on Alexander Hamilton (1755–1804) and the Federalists in the *Gazette* prompted Jefferson to remark that Freneau had "saved our Constitution, which was galloping fast into monarchy." When the *Gazette* went out of business in 1793, Freneau retired to his farm in New Jersey. He perished in a blizzard on December 18, 1832.

G

GAGE, Thomas (1721–1787). A professional soldier, Gage was the last royal governor of Massachusetts. He was sent to America in 1754 and served under the British commander Edward Braddock (1695–1755) during the disastrous attack on Fort Duquesne in 1755. He also served under Jeffrey Amherst (1717–1797) during the final conquest of French Canada in 1760 and was military governor of Montreal for a time. Gage succeeded Amherst as commander in chief of the British forces in North America in 1763 and continued in this capacity for the next 10 years. In 1774, he was appointed governor of Massachusetts, replacing Thomas Hutchinson (1711–1780) at a time of serious unrest. Leading radicals, such as Samuel Adams (1722–1803) and **John Hancock** (*see*), were trying to stir up unrest between the colonists and the government. Gage was also faced with the duty of enforcing the punitive Boston Port Act of 1774. In open defiance of British rule, the colonists formed a Provincial Congress at Concord to govern Massachusetts. Gage's raids on colonial military supplies in Lexington and Concord on April 19, 1775, became the first battles of the Revolution. As a result, Gage was severely criticized in London for military inefficiency. He resigned the same year and sailed for England, where he died in 1787.

GATES, Horatio (1728?–1806). Gates was praised as a hero when American troops under his command defeated **John Burgoyne** (*see*) in 1777 during the Saratoga campaign. He was called a fool three years later, after his army

Horatio Gates

was routed by **Charles Cornwallis** (*see*) at Camden, South Carolina. Born in England, Gates joined the British army at an early age and saw duty in America during the French and Indian War (1754–1763). He was severely wounded in 1755 during the battle for Fort Duquesne. He retired from the British army in 1765 and seven years later immigrated to Virginia at the urging of his friend, **George Washington** (*see*). Gates was commissioned a brigadier general in 1775 and appointed adjutant general of the Continental Army. The following year he was assigned to duty in the Northern Department, covering New York State, under **Philip Schuyler** (*see*). After American setbacks in Canada, Gates replaced Schuyler as commander. The defeat of Burgoyne's army at Saratoga in 1777 advanced Gates' career, although the military skill of **Benedict Arnold** (*see*) was largely responsible for the victory. The Second Continental Congress made Gates president of the Board of War. While serving in this post, Gates became indirectly involved in one of the most scandalous episodes of the American Revolution. One of his aides, **James Wilkinson** (*see*), reputedly disclosed that an embittered general, **Thomas Conway** (*see*), was unsuccessfully agitating to have Washington replaced as the commander in chief. Gates, who many thought should succeed Washington, was implicated but denied any involvement. In 1780, he was given command in the Carolina theater. In a fierce engagement with British regulars under Cornwallis, Gates' poorly trained army was smashed at Camden on August 16, 1780. It was one of America's most costly defeats. Gates was severely criticized, and he was replaced by **Nathanael Greene** (*see*). Congress ordered an investigation but later dropped the matter. Gates eventually settled in New York, where he served in the New York legislature (1800–1801).

GEORGE III (1738–1820). This king of Great Britain was responsible for most of the repressive acts and policies that provoked the American Revolution. Upon succeeding his grandfather, George II (1683–1760), in 1760, George III set out to strengthen the power of the throne and weaken the influence of his opponents in Parliament. He especially aroused resentment in America early in his reign by sponsoring the restrictive Stamp Act of 1765.

George III

George suffered a brief attack of insanity during the same year, but the incident was kept secret. (Modern medical research has indicated that he might have suffered deliriums caused by porphyria, a disease common among the royal families of Europe.) In 1770, the king appointed **Frederick North** (*see*) to be his prime minister. For the next 12 years, Lord North carried out the king's oppressive policies. The Boston Tea Party in 1773 angered George so much that he determined to punish the American colonies. Ignoring the advice of such statesmen as **Charles Fox** and **Edmund Burke** (*see both*), he instituted a policy to subdue the colonies. George suffered recurrent attacks of insanity after 1780, and by 1811 he was blind. His eldest son, later George IV (1762–1830), acted as regent during the last nine years of his reign.

GLOVER, John (1732–1797). Glover, a prosperous merchant from the Massachusetts seaport of Marblehead, was in charge of transporting George Washington's army across the East River to Manhattan after the defeat at the Battle of Long Island in August, 1776. He was also responsible for ferrying Washington's men across the Delaware River on the night of December 25, 1776, before the American victory the next day at the Battle of Trenton. Glover was a member of the Marblehead Committee of Correspondence before the war and was selected after the Revolution broke out to organize the local defense forces. He subsequently joined Washington and was put in charge of equipping and supplying armed vessels for the defense of the colonies. He was forced to retire from service in 1782 because of ill health. He

later served on the Massachusetts General Court (1788–1789).

GREEN MOUNTAIN BOYS. This irregular regiment, made up of settlers from west of the Green Mountains in present-day Vermont, fought in several decisive battles of the Revolution. It was first formed in 1770 as a guerrilla unit to defend the settlers' claims against New York land speculators. Vermont was claimed by New Hampshire, which in 1749 began granting town charters in the area that became known as the New Hampshire Grants. When **George III** (*see*) of England declared in 1764 that Vermont belonged to New York, the settlers began arming themselves to repel land agents from New York. **Ethan Allen** (*see*) and his brothers helped to organize the irregulars in 1770. Named the Green Mountain Boys, they terrorized New York land agents. At the outbreak of the Revolution in 1775, the Green Mountain Boys, under Allen's command, captured Fort Ticonderoga and subsequently seized control of Lake Champlain. Pleased with their victories, the Second Continental Congress awarded the Vermont irregulars the same pay as Continental soldiers. Allen then led his men on an expedition to capture Montreal and was himself captured instead. In 1777, while Allen was still a prisoner, the regiment participated in the victory at Saratoga. That same year, the settlers proclaimed Vermont an independent republic. On Allen's release in 1778, a border war with New York flared up. Allen tried to get the Continental Congress to grant statehood, but the land dispute was not settled until 1791, when New York dropped its claims and Vermont became the 14th state in the Union.

Nathanael Greene

GREENE, Nathanael (1742–1786). Often ranked second to George Washington as a military strategist, Greene commanded American forces in the South after 1780 and liberated the Carolinas and Georgia from British control. Born in Warwick, Rhode Island, Greene was a Quaker until he was expelled from that sect in 1773 for attending a military parade. He then joined the Rhode Island militia and quickly rose from private to brigadier. As a brigadier general in the Continental Army, he commanded the patriots at the siege of Boston (1775–1776) and took charge of the city after the British withdrew. During the next two years, Greene served in the Battles of Trenton, Brandywine, Germantown, and Monmouth. He was appointed quartermaster general in 1778, and two years later succeeded **Horatio Gates** (*see*) as commander of the Southern Army. At the time, the Carolinas were under the control of British forces, which had seized Charleston in

1780. Although **Charles Cornwallis** (*see*) defeated Greene at Guilford Court House, near modern Greensboro, North Carolina, in 1781, his victory was costly and indecisive. The British commander was forced to retire to the coast and moved north to Yorktown, Virginia. By December, 1781, only Charleston remained in British hands. It was finally freed in 1782. After the war, Greene settled in Georgia.

H

HALE, Nathan (1755–1776). This 21-year-old American officer became known as the Martyr Spy of the Revolution. He was born in Coventry, Connecticut. He graduated from Yale in 1773 and became a schoolteacher. After the Battle of Lexington in 1775, Hale enlisted in the Continental Army. He was made a lieutenant and took part in the siege of Boston.

After being promoted to captain on January 1, 1776, Hale served in the Long Island campaign, which was going poorly for the Americans. When George Washington asked for a volunteer to spy on the British, Hale offered his services. On or about September 12, 1776, Hale left the American camp at Harlem Heights on Manhattan, and disguised as a Dutch schoolmaster, penetrated the enemy lines on Long Island. He accomplished his mission, hid the military information in his boots, and was returning to the American lines when he was captured by the British on September 21. Hale was taken before **Sir William Howe** (*see*), who sentenced him to hang the following morning without a trial. His last words were, "I only regret that I have but one life to lose for my country."

HANCOCK, John (1737–1793). Hancock was the first signer of

Moments before his execution, Hale glares defiantly at British troops.

John Hancock

the **Declaration of Independence** (*see*). Because he wrote so large, his name has become synonymous with the word signature. Hancock was born in Braintree (now Quincy), Massachusetts. After his father, a minister, died, he was adopted by his uncle, Thomas Hancock (1703–1764), a wealthy merchant. After graduating from Harvard in 1754, he entered his uncle's shipping business in Boston. When his uncle died in 1764, Hancock became one of the richest men in the American colonies. He was elected to the Massachusetts legislature in 1766 and served until 1772. He became a leading advocate of resistance to England after his sloop, the *Liberty,* was seized in 1768 by customs officials, who charged him with smuggling. British efforts to arrest Hancock and Samuel Adams (1722–1803), who was the leading colonial propagandist, led to the Battles of Lexington and Concord on April 19, 1775. Hancock was elected president of the Second Continental Congress that same year but resigned the office in 1777 after he was denied command of the Continental Army. In 1778, he led an unsuccessful expedition against the British on Rhode Island. Although Hancock's vanity and ambition often led to quarrels with

other patriots, he was very popular in Massachusetts and was elected governor nine times between 1780 and 1793.

HAYS, Mary Ludwig. *See* **Molly Pitcher.**

HERKIMER, Nicholas (1728–1777). This prosperous New York farmer and revolutionary officer commanded the militia in the crucial Battle of Oriskany on August 6, 1777. His troops suffered heavy losses when they were ambushed by a combined force of Indians and pro-British settlers led by **Joseph Brant** and **Sir John Johnson** (*see both*). Herkimer himself sustained a leg wound that soon cost him his life. But the battle—and the rumors of American reinforcements under **Benedict Arnold** (*see*)—ended the British siege of Fort Stanwix by **Barry St. Leger** (*see*), who was thus prevented from joining the British general **John Burgoyne** (*see*) for the invasion of the Hudson Valley.

HESSIANS. This was the popular name given to the 30,000 German mercenaries hired by the British to fight in America during the Revolution. They were called Hessians because about 17,000 of them had been hired from the German state of Hesse-Kassel (*see p. 240*). The Hessians, who were expertly drilled, were led by German officers. They participated in nearly all the campaigns and battles of the war. When taken prisoner by the Americans, the Hessians were treated better than captured British soldiers. George Washington's defeat of the Hessians (*see p. 214*) at the Battle of Trenton on December 26, 1776, helped to boost the morale of the then inexperienced American troops. After the war, about half

the surviving Hessians returned to Germany. Many had deserted to the American side, and a large number settled in America. Most became farmers or artisans.

HOPKINS, Esek (1718–1802). Hopkins was the first commander of the Continental Navy. Born on a Rhode Island farm, he went to sea shortly after his father's death in 1738. He commanded a privateer during the French and Indian War (1754–1763). In 1775, the newly formed Marine Committee of the Second Continental Congress, of which his brother, Stephen Hopkins (1707–1785), was an influential member, made him commander in chief of the navy. The Continental Navy consisted of eight converted merchant ships, the largest carrying only 24 guns. In February, 1776, Hopkins led his small fleet to the Bahamas. Serving aboard his flagship, the *Alfred,* was **John Paul Jones** (*see*). The Americans captured a British supply base on the island of New

Hessian troops also carried pikes and wore a variety of colorful uniforms.

Esek Hopkins

Providence. However, on the return voyage, the fleet met the 20-gun English corvette *Glasgow*. After a three-hour battle in which a number of Hopkins' ships were badly damaged, the English ship escaped. On reaching New London, Hopkins had to discharge a large number of his men because of wounds and disease. He was criticized for permitting the *Glasgow* to escape. Hopkins was unable to overcome the difficulties of refitting his squadron, and his fleet was blockaded in Narragansett Bay by the British in December. Congress, angered at his inaction, dismissed him from the service in 1778. He subsequently served as deputy to the Rhode Island General Assembly until 1786.

HOWE, Sir William (1729–1814). Howe, a veteran of the capture of Quebec in 1759, commanded British forces in the American Revolution for three years but failed to defeat **George Washington** (*see*) decisively. He was sent to Boston in 1775 with reinforcements for **Thomas Gage** (*see*) and served as Gage's second in command. Howe personally led the assault on Breed's Hill during the Battle of Bunker Hill. Shortly afterward, he succeeded Gage as commander in chief of all British forces in North America. He withdrew his troops from Boston in 1776 and that same year won the Battles of Long Island and White Plains (*see pp. 211–213*), driving Washington's army from New York and New Jersey. He again defeated Washington at Brandywine and Germantown, Pennsylvania, in 1777 and took control of Philadelphia. Despite his victories, Howe was not able to end American resistance. He complained that the British government did not provide him with enough support and resigned his command in 1778. He was replaced by **Sir Henry Clinton** (*see*). Howe subsequently held various commands and political posts in England until his death on July 12, 1814.

J

JEFFERSON, Thomas (1743–1826). Statesman, philosopher, and President, Jefferson was born in a simple home in what is now Albemarle County, Virginia. His father was a magistrate, and his mother was a member of the Virginia aristocracy. When Jefferson was 14, his father died, leaving him 2,700 acres of land and a number of slaves. In later life, Jefferson's holdings increased to some 10,000 acres of land and at least 100 slaves. In 1760, Jefferson entered the College of William and Mary. While there, he was greatly influenced by Professor William Small (?–1775). Small helped Jefferson develop what would become his lifelong interest in science. In 1767, Jefferson became a lawyer, but he was a poor public speaker and disliked arguing cases in court. During his first year in the legal profession, Jefferson moved to the site, three miles outside of Charlottesville, where his famous home, Monticello, would later be built. In 1769, Jefferson was elected to the Virginia House of Burgesses and served in it until 1775. He married Martha Wayles Skelton, a wealthy widow, in 1772. Six children were born to the couple, but only two daughters, Mary and Martha, survived childhood. In 1774, Jefferson wrote *A Summary View of the Rights of British America.* In this widely read pamphlet, Jefferson argued that Parliament had no authority over the colonies. According to Jefferson, colonial allegiance to the crown was purely voluntary. The following year, Jefferson was elected a member of the Second Continental Congress. On July 2, 1776, it approved the resolution by **Richard Henry Lee** (*see*) calling for the dissolution of all political ties with England. The formal an-

Thomas Jefferson

nouncement of separation, the **Declaration of Independence** (*see*), was written by Jefferson, who was selected to prepare it because of what John Adams (1735–1826) called his "peculiar felicity of expression." It was adopted on July 4, 1776. The ideas it contained were not new. As he later wrote, he meant the Declaration to be "an expression of the American mind." In September, 1776, Jefferson returned home to Virginia. That same year, as a member of the Virginia House of Delegates, Jefferson wrote a Bill for Establishing Religious Freedom, in which he asserted that a government had no right to dictate a person's opinions or beliefs. Jefferson considered this bill, which was finally enacted in 1786, one of his major accomplishments. From 1779 to 1781, Jefferson served as governor of Virginia, succeeding Patrick Henry (1736–1799) in that post. His governorship was filled with difficulties brought on by the British invasion of Virginia. Later that year, Jefferson's administration was investigated by a committee of the Virginia House of Delegates for his alleged failure to repel the invasion effectively. Jefferson was exonerated. That same year, Jefferson was thrown by his horse and retired to Monticello to recuperate. Tired of public life, Jefferson was looking forward to pursuing his private interests. However, the loneliness that resulted from his wife's death in 1782 induced him to return to a career in government. (*Entry continues in Volume 4.*)

JOHNSON, Sir John (1742–1830). A native of the Mohawk Valley in upstate New York, Johnson served as a captain in the militia during Pontiac's rebellion in the early 1760s. For this service and because of his skill in dealing with Indians, he was made a colonel in the state militia. When the Revolution began, Johnson was forced to flee to Montreal because of his pro-British sympathies. In 1777, he joined **Barry St. Leger** (*see*) in New York State at the siege of Fort Stanwix and the Battle of Oriskany. Three years later, he led a large force of Indians and pro-British militia on a devastating sweep through the lower Mohawk Valley. His support of the British and his treatment of the local residents during the war resulted in the confiscation of his property by the New York Assembly in 1779. The British, however, rewarded him with land in Canada and the title Superintendent General and Inspector General of the Six Nations Indians and those in the Province of Quebec. He died in Montreal on January 4, 1830.

JONES, John Paul (1747–1792). Scottish-born John Paul Jones was the first American naval hero. His name was originally John Paul. He joined the British merchant marine at the age of 12 and became captain of his own ship 10 years later. In 1773, several of his crew mutinied in the West Indies, and he killed a seaman. He fled to America to avoid trial and took the name of Jones. After joining the small American navy at the start of the Revolution, Jones was given command of the *Ranger* in 1777. He sailed her to France and made daring raids on British ports and shipping from his base in Brest. On one of these raids he attacked Whitehaven, near his old home. In the spring of 1778, Jones captured the H.M.S. *Drake,* the first British warship ever to surrender to an American captain. The following year, **Louis XVI**

John Paul Jones

(*see*) placed an old French merchant ship, the *Duras,* under Jones' command. Jones renamed her the **Bonhomme Richard** (*see*). He then sailed for British waters with four other ships and two French privateers. All but one of these ships, the *Pallas,* deserted him. At sunset on September 23, Jones sighted a convoy of British merchant ships in the North Sea off the Yorkshire coast. They were escorted by two British warships, the *Serapis* and the *Countess of Scarborough.* Jones ran the bow of the *Bonhomme Richard* into the stern of the *Serapis,* while the *Pallas* successfully engaged the other warship. Jones' ship suffered severe damage below the waterline and caught fire in several places (*see pp. 224–225*). However, when the captain of the *Serapis* asked him if he was ready to surrender, Jones replied, "I have not yet begun to fight." The battle lasted for three and a half hours, until the *Serapis* finally surrendered. Because his own ship was slowly sinking, Jones transferred to the *Serapis* and sailed his prize to Holland. In 1788, Jones joined the Russian navy and served as a rear admiral in a war against Turkey. He retired in Paris in 1790.

K

KALB, Johann (1721–1780). Kalb, who was born in Germany, was a French army officer who came to America to serve with the Continental Army. Born a peasant, he adopted the title Baron de Kalb to promote his military career. He fought as an officer in both the War of the Austrian Succession (1740–1748) and the Seven Years War (1756–1763). After the outbreak of the American Revolution, Kalb and the **Marquis de Lafayette** (*see*) were encouraged by **Silas Deane** (*see*) to fight in America. Kalb arrived in 1777 and was made a major general. He spent that winter at **Valley Forge** (*see*). In 1780, Kalb took part in an expedition under **Horatio Gates** (*see*) to lift the British siege of Charleston, South Carolina. On August 16, at the Battle of Camden, he charged the British three times without success. He was wounded 11 times and died three days later.

KNOX, Henry (1750–1806). Knox was one of the outstanding military leaders of the Revolution. He took part in nearly every important battle of the war. He volunteered for service under **Artemas Ward** (*see*) at the start of the Revolution and soon became a valued adviser to George Washington. Knox directed Washington's crossing of the Delaware

Henry Knox

River on December 25, 1776, and participated in the Battle of Trenton the next day. He was afterward commissioned a brigadier general and fought with distinction at Brandywine, Germantown, Monmouth, and Yorktown. A key figure in the establishment of West Point in 1778, Knox was named its commander four years later. He organized the **Society of the Cincinnati** (*see*) in 1783. Knox was appointed Secretary of War in 1785 and continued in that post under President George Washington until 1794. He later settled in present-day Maine.

KOSCIUSKO, Thaddeus (1746–1817). Kosciusko, a Polish patriot and military engineer who came to America to join the Continental Army, was instrumental in the success of the Saratoga campaign in 1777. Kosciusko left Poland in 1769 to study engineering and artillery in France. Upon his arrival in America in 1776, he designed fortifications along the Delaware River. He was made a

colonel of engineers in the Continental Army that same year. Kosciusko served under **Horatio Gates** (*see*), and his fortifications and choice of battlefields helped to bring about the defeat of John Burgoyne's forces at Saratoga in 1777. In 1778, he supervised the building of fortifications at West Point. He was in charge of transportation during the strategic retreat of **Nathanael Greene** (*see*) to Virginia in 1781. In 1784, Kosciusko, now a brigadier general, returned to Poland. In 1794, he led an uprising and became dictator of Poland, but he was soon deposed by the Russians. Kosciusko visited America three years later. He continued to fight for

Thaddeus Kosciusko

Polish independence until his death in Switzerland in 1817.

L

LAFAYETTE, Marquis de. Title of Marie Joseph Paul Yves Roch Gilbert du Motier (1757–1834). The Marquis de Lafayette, a French soldier and statesman, valiantly served the American cause during the Revolution. The son of a French colonel, Lafayette inherited a large fortune from his grandfather and joined the French army when he was 13 years old. In 1776, he volunteered to serve in the Continental Army and was commissioned a major general by the Second Continental Congress the following year. On his arrival in America, Lafayette became a close friend of **George Washington** (*see*) and spent the winter of 1777–1778 at **Valley Forge** (*see*). In October, 1778, the "soldier's friend," as Lafayette was called by American troops, returned to France to try to recruit aid for America. Largely through his efforts, **Louis XVI** (*see*) sent a French army under the command of **Count de Rochambeau** (*see*) to assist the Americans. Lafayette returned to America in 1780 and served as a liaison between Rochambeau and Washington. Troops led by Lafayette played a key role in the American victory at the Battle of Yorktown on October 19, 1781. Lafayette returned to Paris that same year. He visited America again in 1784. In France, Lafayette became an active supporter of the French Revolution, serving as one of the leaders of the National Guard. He sent Washington the key to the Bastille, the prison in Paris whose seizure on July 14, 1789, marked the beginning of the Revolution. When radicals took over the French government, Lafayette, a moderate, was branded a traitor and forced to flee France in 1792. He eventually went to Austria, then at war with France, and was imprisoned for five years. Lafayette returned to France in 1799 and went into semiretirement until 1815. In that year, he became a member of the French Chamber of Deputies. Lafayette was acclaimed on a tour of America in

CARNAVALET, BULLOZ

Marquis de Lafayette

1824 and 1825. His grave in Paris is covered with earth taken from Bunker Hill.

LAURENS, Henry (1724–1792). Laurens, a wealthy South Carolina planter, became president of the Second Continental Congress in 1777. He resigned the next year, and in 1780 he was sent to Holland to arrange a treaty and loan on behalf of the United States. Laurens' ship was captured by the British, and he spent a year imprisoned in the Tower of London. He was exchanged for **Charles Cornwallis** (*see*) early in 1782. After his release, Laurens took part in the peace negotiations with Great Britain that resulted in the **Treaty of Paris** (*see*) of September 3, 1783. The following year, Laurens retired to his South Carolina estate.

LEDYARD, William (1738–1781). Ledyard, an American artillery captain, was in command of Fort Griswold outside New London, Connecticut, in 1781, when a British army led by **Benedict Arnold** (*see*) captured the city. Despite a warning by the British that the fort's defenders would be given no quarter, Ledyard refused to surrender. Although the fort was undermanned and undersupplied, it was not captured until the Americans had killed or wounded nearly 200 British soldiers. On entering the fort, the British leader of the attacking force, a Major Bromfield, asked who commanded it. Ledyard replied, "I did, but you do now." Ledyard then surrendered his sword and was immediately killed with it. The remaining Americans in the fort were massacred.

LEE, Charles (1758–1782). An English soldier of fortune, Lee joined the Continental Army, but according to some historians, he was a traitor to the American cause. Lee, a general, was captured in New Jersey in December, 1776, by British troops. While a prisoner, he became a friend of **Sir William Howe** (*see*). He gave Howe a plan to defeat the American army, though it is possible that the plan may have been a ruse. Meanwhile, the Second Continental Congress, unaware of this alleged treason, bargained for Lee's exchange. Freed in 1778, Lee subsequently took part in the Battle of Monmouth on June 28. During this battle, he got into a dispute with George Washington because he had ordered his troops to retreat rather than attack. Washington's own appearance on the field of battle turned a potential American defeat into victory. Washington relieved Lee of his command and later refused the apology that Lee demanded. Lee was quickly court-martialed for disobedience, suspended for a year, and finally dismissed from the army in January, 1780. He died in Philadelphia in 1782.

LEE, Henry (1756–1818). Henry Lee earned the name Light Horse Harry because of the brilliance he displayed as a cavalry leader during the Revolution. In 1777, his Virginia cavalry regiment was assigned to the Continental Army. Despite his youth, Lee quickly distinguished himself and became a close friend and trusted aide of George Washington. Lee later performed brilliantly in the Carolina campaign waged by **Nathanael Greene** (*see*). On March 15, 1781, Greene and Lee were attacked by **Charles Cornwallis** (*see*) at Guilford Court House. Both sides suffered heavy casualties, and Cornwallis was forced to retire to the coast for supplies. The British commander then moved his forces north to Yorktown, where he was defeated. After the war, Lee was a member of the Congress of the Confederation from 1785 to 1788. He was governor of Virginia from 1792 to 1795. Lee was assigned by President Washington in 1794 to put down the Whiskey Rebellion in western Pennsylvania, which he accomplished without any loss of life. He later served a term in the United States Congress (1799–1801). It was Lee who, on the death of Washington in 1799, described him in the House of Representatives as "first in war, first in peace, and first in the hearts of his countrymen." The fifth child of Lee's second marriage was Robert E. Lee (1807–1870), who became the leading Confederate general of the Civil War (1861–1865).

LEE, Richard Henry (1732–1794). Lee, a signer of the **Declaration of Independence** (*see*), was born into an aristocratic Virginia family and was educated in England. He was elected to the Virginia House

Richard Henry Lee

of Burgesses in 1758 and played a prominent role in defending colonial rights. In 1773, Lee, Patrick Henry (1736–1799), and **Thomas Jefferson** (*see*) initiated the intercolonial Committees of Correspondence. As a Virginia delegate to both Continental Congresses, Lee advocated independence. On June 7, 1776, he offered a resolution that the "united colonies" be separated from Great Britain. The resolution, adopted July 2, was quickly followed by the passage of the Declaration of Independence. A signer of the **Articles of Confederation** (*see*), Lee served in the Congress of the Confederation from 1784 to 1789 and was its president for one year. In 1787, Lee opposed ratification of the United States Constitution because it did not contain a bill of rights. His series of "Letters of the Federal Farmer" was used as an argument against ratification. After his election to the United States Senate in 1789, Lee became a strong advocate for the addition of a bill of rights to the Constitution. He resigned because of ill health in 1792 and died two years later in Virginia.

LINCOLN, Benjamin (1733–1810). Lincoln, a Massachusetts farmer who distinguished himself as a general in the early part of the Revolutionary War, was captured with his entire army at Charleston, South Carolina, on May 12, 1780. His surrender was a severe blow to the American cause in the South. Lincoln had been named commander of American forces in the South in 1778, more than a year after he took part in the American victory over **John Burgoyne** (*see*) in the Saratoga campaign. Following the surrender of Charleston, Lincoln was paroled by the British and finally returned to service to take part in the campaign at Yorktown in the fall of 1781. When the British sent out a junior officer to the surrender ceremony, Lincoln was chosen by George Washington to accept officially on behalf of the victorious Americans. In October of that year, he was appointed secretary of war, serving until shortly after the **Treaty of Paris** (*see*) in 1783. Lincoln returned to his farm and became involved in unsuccessful land speculations in present-day Maine. He was appointed in 1787 to put down Shays' Rebel-

Benjamin Lincoln

lion. He later was a federal commissioner, assigned to negotiate treaties with the Creek Indians in the South in 1789 and with the Indians north of the Ohio River in 1793.

LIVINGSTON, Robert R. (1746–1813). Livingston, a prominent New York lawyer, served with distinction before, during, and after the Revolution. He lost his post as recorder of New York in 1775 because of his revolutionary sympathies. Livingston subsequently was an active member of the Second Continental Congress (*see* **Continental Congress**), serving on many committees that helped conduct the war against Britain. He was one of five men chosen to write the **Declaration of Independence** (*see*) but was absent from Philadelphia at the time the Declaration was signed. As chancellor of New York (1777–1801), Livingston administered the oath of office to President George Washington on April 30, 1789. He later served as minister to France (1801–1804) and is credited with directing the negotiations that led to the Louisiana Purchase in 1803. Livingston was a principal backer of the inventor Robert Fulton (1765–1815), whose first successful steamboat was at one time named the *Clermont* in honor of Livingston's home.

LOUIS XVI (1754–1793). Eight years after his military support of the Americans led to the decisive victory at Yorktown in 1781, Louis XVI of France was himself embroiled in a revolution. Unlike the American Revolution, the French Revolution was an internal struggle between wealthy aristocrats, a growing merchant class, and impoverished peasants. In part to maintain the upkeep on

A citoyen *displays Louis XVI's head to troops of the French Republic.*

his luxurious Palace of Versailles and to finance his support of the American Revolution, Louis levied a series of taxes on his people. As a result, food prices rose so high that many people could not feed their families. On July 14, 1789, French citizens began the French Revolution by capturing the Bastille, an infamous prison in Paris. That October, a large group of workers marched to Versailles and forcibly brought Louis, his wife, Marie Antoinette (1775–1793), and their children to Paris. In June, 1791, Louis and his family tried to escape, but they were captured and placed under guard in Paris. In December, 1792, after France had been declared a republic, Louis XVI was tried and convicted of treason. He was guillotined on January 21, 1793. Marie Antoinette suffered the same fate on October 16, 1793.

M

MARION, Francis (1732?–1795). Marion, the leader of a small guerrilla-warfare unit known as Marion's Brigade, successfully staged hit-and-run attacks against the British during the Revolution (*see pp. 260–268*). He was nicknamed the Swamp Fox by **Sir Banastre Tarleton** (*see*), who commanded the British army that tried to run down Marion and his men in the Carolina swamps in 1780. Marion's force, which seldom numbered more than 200 men, played a vital role in forcing **Charles Cornwallis** (*see*) to retreat north to Yorktown, Virginia, in 1781. Before and after the Revolution, Marion was a planter. He served in the South Carolina senate from 1782 to 1790 and was a member of that state's constitutional convention in 1790.

MARTIN, Josiah (1737–1786). Martin was governor of North Carolina before the Revolution. Loyal to the crown, he fled for his life after hearing the news of the Battle of Lexington in 1775. The son of a British officer and himself a professional soldier for 12 years (1757–1769), Martin was appointed governor in 1771. Acting under royal orders, he resisted the claims of planters and merchants who were trying to confiscate the lands of nonresident debtors. As a result, the colony's judicial system collapsed in 1773. Further dissatisfaction resulted when Martin tried to tax the colonists to finance the emergency courts he set up and when the crown created a boundary line with South Carolina that deprived North Carolina of territory its colonists claimed. In defiance, patriotic leaders, led by **James Moore** (*see*), set up their own Provincial Congress. After fleeing from North Carolina in the spring of 1775, Martin returned with British troops but was defeated at the Battle of Moore's Creek Bridge on February 27, 1776. He subsequently served with both **Sir Henry Clinton** and **Charles Cornwallis** (*see both*) during their campaigns in the Carolinas.

MASON, George (1725–1792). Before becoming a member of the Constitutional Convention in 1787, this Virginia planter was an active opponent of repressive British laws, such as the Stamp Act of 1765. He had also been a member of Virginia's constitutional convention in 1776, during which he wrote much of that colony's Declaration of Rights. The document reflected Mason's concern for state and individual rights and served as a model for other state constitutions. Although a delegate to the Constitutional Convention, Mason refused to sign the United States Constitution and campaigned against its ratification in Virginia. He objected that it lacked a provision for the abolishment of slavery and adequate protection of individual liberties.

MERCER, Hugh (1725?–1777). Mercer, a Scottish-born physician, played a leading role in the American victory at the Battle of

Trenton on December 26, 1776. After serving in the French and Indian War (1754–1763), Mercer moved from his home in Pennsylvania to Virginia. He was commissioned a brigadier general in 1776, shortly after the outbreak of the Revolution. He helped to plan the attack on Trenton and led one of the attacking brigades. On January 3, 1777, Mercer tried to seize the bridge over Stony Brook during the Battle of Princeton. His horse was shot out from under him, and he was bayoneted by the British while trying to rally his men. He died of his wounds nine days later.

MINUTEMEN. Volunteers in the colonial militia who could be relied on to arm themselves at a moment's notice—hence the name Minutemen—played a prominent part in the Battles of Lexington and Concord in 1775. The Minutemen were first formed in 1774 at Worcester when the Massachusetts militia was reorganized to get rid of pro-British members. One-third of the men in the old militia were enlisted in newly created regiments of Minutemen. Gradually, other Massachusetts counties formed companies of Minutemen, most of whom were farmers.

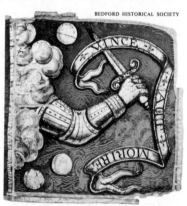

BEDFORD HISTORICAL SOCIETY

"Conquer or Die" was the motto on this Minutemen's banner at Concord.

In the opening hours of the Revolution on April 19, 1775, Minutemen were called to confront the British army on Lexington Common. At Concord, Minutemen joined with local patriots and regular militia to resist the British at the Old North Bridge. Both the militia and Minutemen harassed the British troops on their retreat to Boston. In July, 1775, the Second Continental Congress urged the other colonies to form similar groups. Maryland, New Hampshire, and Connecticut did so.

MOLLY PITCHER. This was the nickname of a revolutionary heroine, Mary Ludwig Hays (1754–1832). The daughter of a Trenton, New Jersey, dairy farmer, she moved to Pennsylvania in 1769 and married John Caspar Hays. In 1775, Hays enlisted in the Continental Army, and Molly eventually went to stay with her parents at Trenton in order to be near him. Hays manned a cannon at the Battle of Monmouth on June 28, 1778. That day was extremely hot, with temperatures nearing 100° F., and Molly, who had accompanied her husband, brought water from a nearby well to the wounded on the battlefield. Her heroic efforts earned her the name Molly Pitcher. Although there is no evidence that she took over her husband's cannon when he fainted from the heat, she did receive a pension in 1822 from the Pennsylvania legislature for supposedly having done so. Another soldier's wife, Margaret Cochrane Corbin (1751–1800), did man a cannon during a battle and became known as Captain Molly. She traveled with her husband John's artillery regiment. After he was killed by **Hessians** (*see*) at the Battle of Fort Washington (northern Manhattan) on Novem-

In the legend, Molly Pitcher manned a cannon after her husband fainted.

MORGAN, Daniel (1736–1802). As commander of a corps of Virginia riflemen, Morgan fought valiantly under **Benedict Arnold** (*see*) in the assault on Quebec in 1775 and helped defeat **John Burgoyne** (*see*) during the Saratoga campaign in 1777. He scored a brilliant victory over **Sir Banastre Tarleton** (*see*) at the Battle of Cowpens, South Carolina, on January 17, 1781. Born in Hunterdon County, New Jersey, Morgan was a rebellious youth. He ran away from home, worked as a laborer, and later fought in the French and Indian War (1754–1763). He became a captain in the Continental Army in 1775 and rose to the rank of brigadier general before retiring to his Virginia plantation in 1781 because of ill health. Morgan returned to duty in 1794 to help put down the short-lived Whiskey Rebellion in western Pennsylvania. He was then appointed military governor of the district and later served a term in the United States Congress (1797–1799).

MORRIS, Robert (1734–1806). Morris, a prosperous Philadelphia merchant and banker, is often referred to as the financier of the American Revolution. Born in England, Morris came to America when he was 13. From 1775 to 1778, he was a member of the Pennsylvania Assembly's delegation to the Second Continental Congress and was a signer of the **Declaration of Independence** (*see*). During the Revolution, Morris served on several Congressional committees and was instrumental in obtaining supplies and money for the army. In February, 1781, when the treasury's lack of funds and credit threatened the progress of the Revolution, Morris was appointed superintendent of finance

ber 16, 1776, she took charge of his gun and fired it until she was severely wounded and captured. In 1799, she became the first woman to be awarded a pension by the United States Congress.

MONTGOMERY, Richard (1738?–1775). This Irish-born revolutionary general was a graduate of Trinity College in Dublin. He went to Canada in 1757 as a British officer in the French and Indian War (1754–1763). After fighting in numerous battles in Canada, New York State, and the West Indies, Montgomery left the army in 1772, settled in New York, and a year later married the daughter of **Robert R. Livingston** (*see*), one of the five men chosen to write the **Declaration of Independence** (*see*). In 1775, he was appointed a brigadier general in the Continental Army, under **Philip Schuyler** (*see*), for the invasion of Canada. When Schuyler became ill, Montgomery assumed complete command and captured

Montreal. In December, 1775, he combined his army with the troops of **Benedict Arnold** (*see*) for the unsuccessful siege of Quebec. Montgomery was killed during an attack on that city (*see p. 208*).

MOORE, James (1737–1777). A wealthy planter, Moore was a patriot leader in North Carolina who fought repressive British trade policies. He was prominent in the Sons of Liberty and in 1774 was the first to sign the call for a Provincial Congress in defiance of the royal governor, **Josiah Martin** (*see*). After the outbreak of the Revolution, Moore directed the colonial forces that defeated Martin and a troop of Scottish Highlanders at the Battle of Moore's Creek Bridge on February 27, 1776. He was made a brigadier general in the Continental Army the next month and given command of all forces in North Carolina. Moore died in April, 1777, while preparing to move his army north to join George Washington.

Robert Morris

by a unanimous vote of Congress. While serving in this capacity for the next three years, Morris obtained a loan from France, persuaded Congress to levy taxes, and established the Bank of North America. He personally financed loans that made possible the defeat of the British at Yorktown on October 19, 1781. After helping to draw up the federal Constitution in 1787, Morris served as United States Senator from Pennsylvania (1789–1795). He lost all his money in land speculations, and in 1798 he was declared bankrupt and sent to debtor's jail, where he remained until 1801. He died in obscurity five years later.

MOULTRIE, William (1730–1805). Moultrie was a revolutionary patriot who led the South Carolina militia in repulsing a British attack on Charleston Harbor on June 28, 1776. Four months later, Moultrie was made a brigadier general in the Continental Army. In 1779, he again successfully defended Charleston against an attempted British invasion of that city. However, on May 12, 1780, Charleston fell, and Moultrie was captured by the British. In February, 1782, he was released

and continued his service in the Continental Army until the end of the war. After the war, Moultrie served as a United States Senator (1787–1791), between two terms as governor of South Carolina (1785–1787 and 1792–1794).

N

NORTH, Frederick (1732–1792). Lord North was prime minister of England before and during the American Revolution. A loyal friend of **George III** (*see*), he carried out the king's repressive measures against the American colonies, even when he disagreed. In 1775, North advised the king not to go to war against the colonists and offered to resign, but George persuaded him to remain in office. However, when North learned that **Charles Cornwallis** (*see*) and his army had surrendered at Yorktown on October 19, 1781, he finally insisted on resigning.

BRITISH MUSEUM

Frederick North

O

OLIVE BRANCH PETITION. In early July, 1775, more than two weeks after the Battle of Bunker Hill, the Second Continental Congress adopted the Olive Branch Petition. It professed the American colonies' loyalty to **George III** (*see*) and asked him to prevent further bloodshed by ceasing all hostilities and repressive measures until a reconciliation could be reached. The petition was written by **John Dickinson** (*see*) and signed by the members of Congress (*see p. 192*). Richard Penn (1735–1811), a descendant of William Penn (1644–1718) and a loyal supporter of Great Britain, was appointed to carry the document to King George. The king would not see Penn nor accept the petition. Instead, he proclaimed that all Americans were disloyal and would be considered rebels by the crown.

P

PAINE, Robert Treat (1731–1814). Paine served as associate prosecuting attorney in the Boston Massacre trial of 1770. He became one of the five representatives from Massachusetts at the First Continental Congress in 1774, and he also served in 1776 in the Second Continental Congress. Paine was one of the few patriots who signed both the **Olive Branch Petition** and the **Declaration of Independence** (*see both*). In 1777, he was elected the first attorney general of Massachusetts. He became a member of the state's supreme court in 1790.

PAINE, Thomas (1737–1809). Paine, who is best known for his

Thomas Paine

pamphlet **Common Sense** (*see*), was a journalist, a political philosopher, and a revolutionary patriot. He was born in Britain and worked for many years as, among other things, a schoolteacher, a grocer, and a tax collector. In 1774, Paine met **Benjamin Franklin** (*see*) in London. That same year, with letters of recommendation from Franklin, he set off for Philadelphia, where he became a journalist. In 1776, Paine wrote *Common Sense,* the pamphlet that effectively and persuasively presented the case for independence from Britain. Over the next several years, he wrote 16 pamphlets that were influential in keeping the revolutionary spirit at a high pitch. After the French Revolution broke out in 1789, Paine went to France, and for the next three years he traveled between London and Paris, advocating worldwide revolution. When **Edmund Burke** (*see*), a member of Parliament, condemned the French Revolution, Paine argued in a pamphlet called *The Rights of Man* (*see*) that men had the right to change their government if it was not responsive to the will of the people. In 1793, the leaders of the French government fell from power. Paine, who had served

with them, was arrested by the radical Committee of Public Safety. He spent a year in prison. During this time, he worked on *The Age of Reason,* a book which dealt with man's relationship to God. Paine believed in God but did not think that the Bible was the word of God. He attacked existing churches because they told people to accept misfortunes that science and government could now eliminate. In 1802, Paine returned to America, where his religious views were considered controversial. Ignored by many of his former friends, Paine lived in poverty until his death in New York on June 8, 1809.

PARKER, Sir Peter (1721–1811). The defeat of this British admiral at Charleston, South Carolina, early in the Revolution resulted in two years of relative peace for the Southern colonies. On June 28, 1776, Parker, with 10 warships and 2,500 men under **Sir Henry Clinton** (*see*), attacked Charleston, the South's most important port. **William Moultrie** (*see*) commanded the fort on Sullivan's Island that guarded the harbor. While Clinton's men tried unsuccessfully to take the fort from the rear, Parker's ships bombarded it from the sea. Moultrie's gunners returned their fire accurately. At sundown, Parker withdrew his shattered fleet from the battle. As a result, the British concentrated their major war efforts on the North. Parker was more successful the next summer when his fleet took part in the British victory in the Battle of Long Island. He became admiral of the fleet in 1799.

PITCAIRN, John (1722–1775). A major in the British royal marines, Pitcairn saw action in the Battles of Lexington and Concord

on April 19, 1775. Pitcairn left his native Scotland in 1756 to accept a captain's commission in the royal marines. He was assigned to the British forces that occupied Boston in 1774. Sent to destroy rebel supplies at Concord, he commanded the British detachment that skirmished with the colonial **Minutemen** (*see*) at Lexington, the first armed clash of the Revolution. Two months later, he was killed while trying to storm the American fortifications at Breed's Hill (*see p. 191*).

PRESCOTT, Samuel (1751–1777?). A physician from Concord, Massachusetts, Prescott may have been the American patriot who successfully completed the midnight ride of **Paul Revere** (*see*) after Revere was stopped by a British cavalry patrol. Prescott had spent the evening of April 18, 1775, in Lexington. On his way home, he met Revere and **William Dawes** (*see*). They had just alerted the residents of Lexington that British troops were advancing on Concord in an effort to capture colonial military supplies and two rebel leaders, Samuel Adams (1722–1803) and **John Hancock** (*see*). Revere invited Prescott to accompany them to Concord. On the way, a British patrol accosted them. Dawes galloped away. Seeing Revere threatened by pistols and swords, Prescott rushed to his aid and tried to hold the British back with his whip. Both Americans were herded into a pasture, when suddenly Prescott yelled "Put on!" jumped his horse over a fence, and escaped. Historians differ as to whether it was he or Dawes who later reached Concord. In 1776, Prescott was captured by the British, apparently at Ticonderoga. He died in prison in Halifax, Canada.

PRIMOGENITURE. One of the many social reforms **Thomas Jefferson** (*see*) worked toward during his three years (1776–1779) in the Virginia House of Delegates was the abolition of the rule of primogeniture. This law entitled only the eldest son to inherit his parents' estate. Primogeniture—a word based on the Latin words for "first" and "birth"—was the legacy of the medieval period in Europe, when the division of great land estates among many heirs would have upset the economic system. By Jefferson's time, New England—with the exception of Rhode Island—had either dropped or modified the law. In Virginia, primogeniture was applied only when the property owner died without a will, although the law in its original form still existed. The complete abolition of primogeniture was one of the 126 reforms that the four-man Board of Revisors, headed by Jefferson, proposed to the Virginia legislature in June, 1778. Most of these reforms became law, but not until after the Revolution. Primogeniture was not abolished in Virginia until 1785. Other states soon followed. In 1798, the last of the original 13 colonies, Rhode Island, also abolished the rule. As a result, more persons were allowed to own property and were thus able to meet qualifications for voting. Since that time, no state in this country has had a primogeniture law.

PULASKI, Casimir (1748?–1779). Pulaski, a restless, headstrong professional soldier who was born in Poland, served in the Continental Army at several major battles during the Revolution. He had been forced to flee his native country in 1772 because of his involvement in an unsuccessful rebellion against the Polish king, Stanislaus II (1732–1798). Pulaski eventually reached Paris, where **Benjamin Franklin** (*see*) persuaded him to join the American cause. Pulaski arrived in Boston in July, 1777, and soon afterward was appointed brigadier general of cavalry in the Continental Army. He distinguished himself at the Battle of Brandywine that September and the next month commanded a small unit in the Battle of Germantown. During the winter of 1777–1778, Pulaski was a cavalry commander and served under **Anthony Wayne** (*see*) in foraging for supplies for the troops at **Valley Forge** (*see*). In March, 1778, however, he resigned his post rather than continue serving under Wayne. He was subsequently given permission to form an independent cavalry unit known as Pulaski's Legion. After serving briefly in New Jersey, the legion was sent to South Carolina, where it suffered a major defeat in May, 1779, during a British attack on Charleston. On October 9, 1779, Pulaski was seriously wounded while leading a cavalry charge against the British at Savannah. He was taken aboard an American ship, on which he died of his injuries two days later.

PUTNAM, Israel (1718–1790). Putnam, a prosperous Connecticut farmer, left his plow and went to war without taking the time to change his clothes when he learned of the Battles of Lexington and Concord in 1775. A veteran of the French and Indian War (1754–1763), he was soon appointed a major general and fought at the Battle of Bunker Hill in 1775 and the Battle of Long Island the following year. Because Putnam preferred to act on his own rather than to obey George Washington's orders, he was relieved of field command and put in charge of the recruiting service in Connecticut. Although later reassigned to the army, he held no important posts. Paralysis ended his military career in 1779.

R

REVERE, Paul (1735–1818). A silversmith and engraver by trade, Revere is best remembered as the horseman who galloped through the countryside to warn the citizens of Lexington and Concord that a British army was coming. The story, embellished in *Paul Revere's Ride* (1863) by poet Henry Wadsworth Longfellow, is only partly true. Two other patriots also rode that night, and Revere was stopped by the British before reaching Concord. Born in Boston, Revere published anti-British propaganda before and during the Revolutionary War. In 1773, he took part in planning the Boston Tea Party. The following year, he was appointed the official messenger of the Massachusetts Provincial Assembly to the First Continental Congress. The night of April 18, 1775, Revere and **William Dawes** (*see*) were sent by **Joseph Warren** (*see*) to spread the news that British troops were on their way to destroy the military supplies at Concord and seize two rebel leaders, Samuel Adams (1722–1803) and **John Hancock** (*see*). Reaching Lexington about midnight, Revere woke the inhabitants and then, accompanied by Dawes and **Samuel Prescott** (*see*), started for Concord. En route, Revere was stopped by a British patrol. His horse was taken away, and he was forced to return to Lexington on foot. One of the two other riders reached

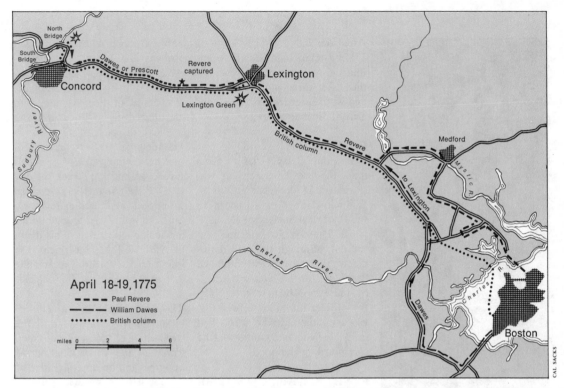

Revere rowed across the Charles River and rode to Lexington with the news that the British were coming. He then headed toward Concord but was stopped by a patrol. Either Dawes or Prescott completed his mission.

Concord, although it is unclear whether it was Dawes or Prescott. Revere subsequently designed and printed the first issue of American money, supervised the manufacture of gunpowder, and created the first official seal of the colonies. As a result of his only military engagement—a poorly planned effort in 1779 to oust the British from Penobscot Bay in present-day Maine—Revere was accused of cowardice and insubordination. At a court-martial three years later, he was cleared of the charges. In later years, Revere became a familiar sight on the streets of Boston, still dressed in the costume of his revolutionary days. The aged silversmith died on May 10, 1818.

RIGHTS OF MAN, THE. This pamphlet by **Thomas Paine** (*see*) was published in two parts in 1791 and 1792 and was widely circulated in the United States and Britain. It was written in reply to *Reflections on the French Revolution,* a pamphlet condemning the French by **Edmund Burke** (*see*). *The Rights of Man,* which was dedicated to George Washington, praised the French and American Revolutions. In it, Paine argued that each generation had the right to make its own laws and should not be bound by the laws of previous generations. According to Paine, government existed to guarantee to all men equally the rights of liberty, property, security, and resistance to oppression. These views stimulated a great deal of controversy in Britain and America. Paine's appeal to the British to overthrow their king led to the issuance of a warrant for his arrest in 1792. He fled to France that same year.

ROCHAMBEAU, Count Jean Baptiste de Vimeur de (1725–1807). Count de Rochambeau, who was chosen by **Louis XVI** (*see*) to command the French army in the American Revolution, was a nobleman with a distinguished military reputation in France. Rochambeau landed in Rhode Island in July, 1780, with an army of 5,500 men. He met **George Washington** (*see*) in September at Hartford, Connecticut. They decided not to attack British-occupied New York until the French could establish naval superiority over Great Britain. In July, 1781, the armies of Rochambeau and Washington were united at White Plains, New York. On September 5, the French fleet defeated the British fleet in Chesapeake Bay. That same month, their troops joined an American force in Virginia led by the **Marquis de Lafayette** (*see*).

Count de Rochambeau

The combined attack against **Charles Cornwallis** (*see*) at Yorktown resulted in a British surrender on October 19, 1781. Two years later, Rochambeau returned to France, where he was active in public and military affairs until his death in 1807.

ROCKINGHAM, Charles Watson-Wentworth (1730–1782). Lord Rockingham was a leading British statesman who disagreed with the repressive policies of **George III** (*see*) toward the American colonies. He became prime minister in 1765, and in an effort to heal differences between Britain and the colonies, repealed the Stamp Act. He was dismissed from office in 1766. During the administration of **Frederick North** (*see*), Rockingham urged Britain to grant the colonies independence.

After the fall of Lord North in 1782, Rockingham became prime minister once again. However, he died after three months in office and was succeeded by the **Second Earl of Shelburne** (*see*).

ROSS, Betsy (1752–1836). The legend that Betsy Griscom Ross made the first American flag was started in 1870 by her grandson, William Canby, in a speech to the Historical Society of Pennsylvania. There is no evidence that she did, although the records indicate that she was employed "making ships' colours, etc." by the Pennsylvania State Navy Board. Her husband, John Ross, was a militiaman who was killed in 1776 when some gunpowder he was guarding exploded.

RUSH, Benjamin (1746–1813). Rush served as the surgeon general of the Continental Army (1777–1778) and as Treasurer of the United States Mint (1797–1813). He was also a member of the Second Continental Congress and one of the signers of the **Declaration of Independence** (*see*). In addition, he founded the American temperance movement and organized the nation's first antislavery society. Rush was born in Pennsylvania and studied medicine at the University of Edinburgh. In 1769, he was appointed to the faculty of the Academy of Philadelphia, becoming the first American professor of chemistry. During the next six years, he became increasingly involved in revolutionary activities in Philadelphia, and he encouraged **Thomas Paine** (*see*) to publish his now famous pamphlet, *Common Sense* (*see*). Rush resigned as surgeon general because of the lack of attention paid to the army's medical service. He later expressed doubts about George Washington's war strategy in letters to leading American figures. Rush subsequently taught medicine at the University of Pennsylvania and established the nation's first free medical dispensary in 1786 in Philadelphia. He was accused of quackery in the wake of a yellow-fever epidemic that struck the city in 1793. He was publicly ridiculed for purging and bleeding fever victims and was forced to give up his medical practice. Before his death on April 19, 1813, Rush helped to found Dickinson College and the first black church in Philadelphia.

RUTLEDGE, Edward (1749–1800). Rutledge, a signer of the **Declaration of Independence** (*see*), served in the First Continental Congress and became a leader of the South Carolina delegation in the Second Continental Congress (*see* **Continental Congress**). He was captured when the British seized Charleston on May 12, 1780, but was later released. Rutledge subsequently proposed a bill in the South Carolina legislature to confiscate the property of colonists loyal to Britain during the Revolution. He was elected governor of South Carolina in 1798 but died before his term was completed.

ST. LEGER, Barry (1737–1789). As an experienced British army officer, Major St. Leger was assigned the task of capturing Fort Stanwix at Rome, New York, after which he was to join **John Burgoyne** (*see*) for the invasion of the Hudson Valley. St. Leger laid siege to the fort and planned the successful ambush of the American militia at Oriskany under **Nicholas Herkimer** (*see*). But the serious losses he suffered in that battle and the erroneous reports of an approaching American force panicked his Indian allies into flight. St. Leger was forced to abandon his attack on the fort and retreat back to Canada, from which he conducted guerrilla warfare against the pro-American settlers in New York. After the war, he served as commander of the British forces in Canada.

SALOMON, Haym (1740?–1785). Emigrating from Poland to the American colonies in 1772, Salomon became a leading financier during the revolutionary period. He opened brokerage houses in New York and Philadelphia and helped maintain American credit by advancing large amounts of cash to the colonial treasury. Salomon handled the war subsidies advanced by the French and Dutch governments and also served as paymaster general of the French troops in America. He was arrested as a spy by the British and condemned to death in 1778, but he managed to escape. Salomon's financial assistance was also extended to individuals, including **Thomas Jefferson** (*see*) and the future fourth President, James Madison (1751–1836).

SCHUYLER, Philip John (1733–1804). Schuyler was one of four major generals appointed in 1775 to serve under George Washington. Born in Albany to a prominent family of Dutch ancestry, Schuyler was a specialist in military supplies and helped to equip the British during the French and Indian War (1754–1763). He served in the New York Assembly (1768–1775) and was a delegate to the First Continental Congress

in 1775 (*see* **Continental Congress**). After assuming command in the New York theater of operations in 1775, Schuyler recruited the army that began its unsuccessful attack on Canada that fall. Illness forced him to yield leadership of the expedition to **Richard Montgomery** (*see*). After Fort Ticonderoga was recaptured by the British in 1777, Schuyler's loyalty and competence were questioned. He asked for a court-martial and was acquitted, but later resigned from the army. Schuyler served (1779–1781) in the Second Continental Congress and also represented New York (1789–1791) in the first United States Senate. He was defeated for reelection by Aaron Burr (1756–1836) but was returned to office in 1797. He retired the following year because of his health. Schuyler's son-in-law was Alexander Hamilton (1755–1804).

SECOND CONTINENTAL CONGRESS. *See* **Continental Congress.**

SHELBURNE, Sir William Petty, Second Earl of (1737–1805). An outspoken critic of the policies of **George III** (*see*), Shelburne signed the **Treaty of Paris** (*see*), which ended the American Revolution in 1783. He had opposed the Stamp Act of 1765 and three years later was forced to resign as secretary of state because of his proposal for a peaceful solution to the colonial problem. After the American victory was assured, Shelburne was asked in 1782 to take office once more under **Charles Rockingham** (*see*). He agreed to do so only on the condition that the king recognize the independence of the new United States. Lord Rockingham died that same year, and Shelburne succeeded him as prime minister. After signing the

peace treaty, his government was defeated the same year by the coalition government of **Frederick North** and **Charles James Fox** (*see both*).

SMALLWOOD, William (1732–1792). A leader of the Maryland Assembly, Smallwood was active in colonial opposition to the British before the Revolution. After war broke out, he raised a regiment of troops that won a reputation for valor at the Battle of Long Island in August, 1776, and covered the Continental Army's subsequent retreat to White Plains, New York. The regiment later fought in several important battles, including those of Trenton and Germantown. Smallwood often complained that he was not promoted as rapidly as he deserved. He also did not like to serve with foreign officers and once threatened to resign rather than serve under **Baron von Steuben** (*see*). After the war, Smallwood served three terms as governor of Maryland (1785–1788).

STARK, John (1728–1822). A veteran of the French and Indian War (1754–1763), Stark immediately volunteered when the Revolution broke out in 1775. He was made a colonel in a regiment of New Hampshire patriots and served at the Battle of Bunker Hill. He subsequently took part in the unsuccessful invasion of Canada in 1776 and at the Battle of Trenton, New Jersey. Stark resigned in March, 1777, because other officers had been promoted over his head. However, when **John Burgoyne** (*see*) invaded New York in an attempt to cut off New England from the other colonies, Stark was made a brigadier general of the New Hampshire troops assembled to aid Vermont against

Steuben drills American soldiers during the winter at Valley Forge.

fought against the British on Staten Island, New York, and then again at the Battle of Germantown in Pennsylvania. He spent the winter of 1777–1778 at **Valley Forge** (*see*). On August 29, 1779, Sullivan routed a combined Indian and loyalist force commanded by **John Butler** (*see*) in the Battle of Newtown, New York. He resigned his commission later that year because of ill health. Returning to New Hampshire, Sullivan subsequently served as attorney general (1782–1786), governor (1786, 1787, and 1789), and United States district judge (1789–1795).

raids by Burgoyne. He defeated a British force of 500 troops outside Bennington, Vermont, on August 16, 1777. As he led his men into action, Stark reportedly told them, "There, my boys, are your enemies, the red-coats and tories; you must beat them or my wife sleeps a widow tonight." Stark later helped to bring about the surrender of Burgoyne's army at Saratoga on October 17, 1777. After the war, he retired to his farm in New Hampshire.

STEUBEN, Baron Friedrich Wilhelm von (1730–1794). Steuben was inspector general of the Continental Army and played an important role in training the inexperienced American troops. The son of a Prussian officer, he enlisted in the Prussian army when he was about 16 years old. At the time of his discharge in 1763, Steuben was a captain. Although an expert in military training, organization, and discipline, he was unable to secure a permanent military appointment in Europe. After meeting **Benjamin Franklin** (*see*) in Paris, Steuben sailed for America in 1777 with a letter of

introduction to **George Washington** (*see*). He was subsequently commissioned by the Second Continental Congress and joined Washington at Valley Forge in February, 1778. Appointed inspector general, Steuben drilled American troops so successfully that he was soon promoted to major general. The value of his training methods was confirmed on June 28, 1778, at the Battle of Monmouth, when Steuben was able to rally the retreating troops of **Charles Lee** (*see*). Three years later, his knowledge of siege warfare was a major factor in Washington's decisive victory at Yorktown, where Steuben commanded a division. Steuben became an American citizen in 1783 and settled in New York State.

SULLIVAN, John (1740–1795). Sullivan, a native of New Hampshire, gained fame as a revolutionary general. He served through the siege of Boston, which lasted from October, 1775, to March, 1776. He was captured by the British at the Battle of Long Island in August, 1776, but was released the same year. In 1777, Sullivan

SUMTER, Thomas (1734–1832). Known as the Gamecock of the Revolution, Sumter was a vigorous leader of guerrilla forces against the British in the Carolinas. His most noted exploits took place after the British conquered South Carolina in 1780. Sumter rallied the colonists and revived resistance to the British. He raised a troop of mounted soldiers by promising them slaves and plunder from settlers loyal to Great Britain. The plan became known as Sumter's law and created legal difficulties for years after the war. Sumter later served in the House of Representatives (1789–1793 and 1797–1801) and the United States Senate (1801–1810).

T

TARLETON, Sir Banastre (1754–1833). Tarleton, a ruthless British officer (*see p. 267*) who commanded a mixed force of cavalry and infantry in the Revolution, served with **Charles Cornwallis** (*see*) in operations in New Jersey and in the seizure of Philadelphia in 1777. Following the capture of Charleston in 1780, Tarleton's Green Horse, as his dragoons were known, brutally wiped out an American force at Waxhaws, South Carolina. The battle brought Tarleton the nickname of The Butcher. He then launched an unsuccessful search for the elusive **Francis Marion** (*see*) in the South Carolina swamps. Tarleton was defeated by **Daniel Morgan** (*see*) at the Battle of Cowpens in South Carolina on January 17, 1781. Tarleton avoided capture and was with the main British army that surrendered nine months later at Yorktown. After his return to England, he served in Parliament (1790–1806 and 1807–1812) and wrote an account of his military campaigns in the South.

TREATY OF PARIS. The American Revolution officially ended with the signing of the Treaty of Paris between Great Britain and the United States on September 3, 1783. At the same time, Britain signed separate peace treaties with two other belligerents—France, an ally of America, and Spain, an ally of France. Negotiations to end the war were started in March, 1782, and a general armistice took effect on January 2, 1783. The lengthy peace talks were complicated by the number of compromises that had to be worked out between the nations involved. The United States was represented in the negotiations by **Benjamin Franklin** (*see*), John Adams (1735–1826), John Jay (1745–1829), and **Henry Laurens** (*see*). Under the terms of the Treaty of Paris, the independence of America was recognized, and boundaries were established that gave America control over all lands south of Canada, as far west as the Mis-

sissippi River and as far south as Florida. An important provision was that Americans were held responsible for paying debts owed to British merchants before the war. One of the causes of the War of 1812 with Britain was the American failure to pay these debts.

TRUMBULL, John (1756–1843). Trumbull, who served with **George Washington** and **Horatio Gates** (*see both*), later painted the most famous visual records of the American Revolution. He was the youngest child of Jonathan Trumbull (1710–1785), a governor of Connecticut. At the outbreak of the war, the governor obtained an appointment for his son in the Continental Army. Trumbull became an aide-de-camp to Washington and later served as a colonel under Gates. He left the army to study art in Boston in 1777 and three years later began studying with the American-born **Benjamin West** (*see*) in London. Following West's "grand historical style" (*see p. 257*), Trumbull turned to contemporary history for subject matter. By 1786, he had painted some of his best works at West's

studio, including "Battle of Bunker's Hill" (*see p. 191*) and "The Death of General Montgomery in the Attack of Quebec" (*see p. 208*). He also painted "Surrender of Lord Cornwallis at Yorktown" and "Declaration of Independence" (*see pp. 201–202*). The last painting was inaccurate: Thirteen signers of the Declaration were omitted, and four persons who did not sign were represented. Trumbull's portrayals of British defeats were not popular in England, and the artist finally returned to New York in 1789. He moved to Philadelphia three years later and while there painted Washington's portrait. In 1793, Trumbull entered the diplomatic service as private secretary to John Jay (1745–1829) in London. He resumed painting on his return to America in 1804. In 1817, Congress commissioned Trumbull to paint four large murals in the rotunda of the Capitol, and these were finished in 1824. Trumbull helped to establish the Trumbull Gallery at Yale in 1832 and donated his art collection to it. The paintings are now in the Yale Gallery of Fine Arts, New Haven, Connecticut.

Trumbull founded America's first college art museum at Yale in 1832.

V

VALLEY FORGE. Situated on the Schuylkill River in southeastern Pennsylvania, Valley Forge was the site chosen by **George Washington** (*see*) to quarter his army during the winter of 1777–1778. The Continental Army arrived there on December 19. It had been forced to retreat following the Battle of Germantown on October 4 and the subsequent British seizure of Philadelphia. The winter at Valley Forge was unusually severe, and the soldiers endured many hardships. They lacked adequate shelter, food, clothing, and medical supplies. It has been estimated that as many as 3,000 of the nearly 11,000 troops died. Many deserted to the British, and at times Washington's officers feared that a mutiny might break out. Nevertheless, the patriotism of the remaining troops and Washington's inspired leadership enabled them to survive the winter. The arrival of **Baron von Steuben** (*see*) in February helped to raise their morale. He immediately began drilling the troops and organizing them into fighting units. America's alliance with France in May, 1778, brought welcome supplies of weapons, clothing, and money. On June 19, 1778, after six months in camp, the army left Valley Forge to pursue the British. The campsite is now a state park.

VON STEUBEN, Baron Friedrich. *See* **Steuben.**

W

WARD, Artemas (1727–1800). Ward directed the siege of Boston for several weeks, until **George Washington** (*see*) arrived to take over command on July 3, 1775. A veteran of the French and Indian War (1754–1763), Ward served in the Massachusetts General Court for many years, although his opposition to royal authority angered colonial officials. Ward was ill when the Battle of Lexington was fought on April 19, 1775. Nevertheless, he rode to Cambridge the next day and took command of the Massachusetts militia there. On May 19, he was commissioned a general and made commander in chief of the Massachusetts troops. He immediately began training the militia into an effective fighting force. He helped to plan the American defenses for the Battle of Bunker Hill. On June 17, 1775, he was appointed a major general in the Continental Army by the Second Continental Congress. On March 4 of the following year, Ward directed the successful assault on Dorchester Heights, which forced the British to evacuate Boston. Shortly afterward, he was forced to resign because of ill health. Ward served in the Second Continental Congress from 1780 to 1781.

WARREN, Joseph (1741–1775). An advocate of American independence, Warren was born and raised in Massachusetts. After graduating from Harvard College in 1759, he became a well-known physician in Boston. Warren actively opposed British exploitation of the colonies and was once described as "the greatest incendiary in all America." His associates included John Adams (1735–1826), **John Hancock** (*see*), and James Otis (1725–1783). Warren was a member of many colonial organizations, including the Massachusetts Committee of Safety. He served as temporary president of that colony's Provincial Congress in 1775. On April 18 of that year, he sent **William Dawes** and **Paul Revere** (*see both*) to Lexington to

For shelter, the American troops at Valley Forge built crude log huts.

warn Hancock and Samuel Adams (1722–1803) of British plans to arrest them. He then helped to organize a Massachusetts militia and was elected a major general on June 14, 1775. Learning of the impending battle at Breed's Hill three days later, Warren volunteered to fight in a noncommand status. He was killed (*see p. 191*) during a British attack.

WASHINGTON, George (1732–1799).

The leadership and military skill exercised by George Washington as commander in chief of the Continental Army was probably the most important factor in the success of the American Revolution. Washington was born in Westmoreland County, Virginia, the son of a prosperous planter. His father died in 1743, and his half brother Lawrence (1718–1752) was responsible for most of George's education. After Lawrence's death, Washington inherited the family estate at Mount Vernon in 1761. A giant for his time, he was more than six feet tall. Washington showed a talent for surveying and in 1749 was made official surveyor of Culpeper County in northern Virginia. In 1753, acting Governor Robert Dinwiddie (1693–1770) of Virginia sent Washington, a major in the colonial militia, to caution the French against violating British claims in the Ohio Valley. The warning was ignored, and Washington was ordered to dislodge the intruders by force. His expedition of 1754 was unsuccessful, but he gained valuable military experience. He saw further action in the French and Indian War (1754–1763), during which he served as aide-de-camp to Edward Braddock (1695–1755) in the disastrous expedition against the French at Fort Duquesne in

George Washington

1755. That same year he was appointed commander of all Virginia militia. In 1758, Washington met Martha Dandridge Custis (1731–1802), a wealthy widow with two children. They were married in January, 1759. The couple had no children of their own. Washington served in the Virginia House of Burgesses from 1759 to 1774. He vigorously opposed the Stamp Act of 1765 and represented Virginia in both Continental Congresses. When armed hostilities with the British began in 1775, Washington, now well-known for his military ability and his integrity, was appointed head of the Continental Army. He assumed command at Cambridge, Massachusetts, on July 3, 1775. His army, although lacking in supplies and poorly trained, was surprisingly effective. After a long siege, Boston was liberated on March 17, 1776. After the Battle of Long Island in August, 1776, Washington was forced to retreat from superior forces under **Sir William Howe** (*see*) and conducted a skillful withdrawal into New Jersey. After winning battles at Trenton on December 26, 1776, and at Princeton eight days later, Washington continued to with-

draw his army, heading into Pennsylvania. There he was defeated at Brandywine and Germantown in the fall of 1777. When the British subsequently occupied Philadelphia, Washington wintered his exhausted troops at **Valley Forge** (*see*). During this period, a discontented general, **Thomas Conway** (*see*), suggested secretly that Washington be replaced by **Horatio Gates** (*see*). However, the unsuccessful plot—known as the Conway Cabal—was exposed. The alliance with France in 1778 brought needed supplies and money to the colonial cause, but it did not immediately affect the course of the war. Washington had to wait two years before enough French troops arrived to go on the offensive. At that point, he and the French commander, **Count de Rochambeau** (*see*), decided not to storm the British stronghold at New York City. Instead, they agreed to shift their operations to the South. On October 19, 1781, with naval and military assistance from the French, Washington defeated **Charles Cornwallis** (*see*) at Yorktown. This was the last major battle of the war. The British army evacuated New York and sailed for home in 1783. Washington had refused pay during his eight years of military service. He had also rejected suggestions that he seize power and declare himself king. He resigned his commission on December 23, 1783, and retired to his plantation at Mount Vernon. (*Entry continues in Volume 4.*)

WAYNE, Anthony (1745–1796).

Wayne, a revolutionary general, was known as Mad Anthony because of his daring military exploits. He was born in Pennsylvania and was a tanner by trade. At the outbreak of the Revolution in 1775, Wayne organized a regiment in Pennsylvania. Commissioned as a colonel, Wayne covered the retreat of the army led by **Benedict Arnold** (*see*) from Canada in 1776. Afterward, he commanded Fort Ticonderoga, where he won his nickname. In 1777, Wayne fought at the Battle of Brandywine. In 1780, after hearing news of Arnold's attempt to betray West Point, Wayne moved his troops to reinforce the post. He settled permanently in Georgia after the war and served one term (1791–1792) in the United States Congress. President George Washington later sent Wayne to deal with the Indian problem in the Northwest Territory (north of the Ohio River). He decisively defeated the Indians at the Battle of Fallen Timbers, near present-day Toledo, on August 20, 1794. He then negotiated an effective peace treaty with the Indians. The victory opened the Ohio region for settlement.

Benjamin West

WEST, Benjamin (1730–1813). West, who trained many American artists at his London studio, was a major influence in the development of American art. Born near Springfield, Pennsylvania, West began painting at an early age. According to legend, he was taught by Indians how to make paints from colored clays, and he made paintbrushes from his brother's hair. When he was about 18, West moved to Philadelphia, where he attended college and earned a living painting portraits and tavern signs. In 1760, he went to Italy to continue his studies. Three years later, he opened a studio in London and was an immediate success. **George III** (*see*) appointed West to the Royal Academy in 1768, and in 1772 he made him "historical" court painter. Among others, West taught Gilbert Stuart (1755–1828) and **John Trumbull** (*see*), and he sponsored **John Singleton Copley** (*see*). The subjects of West's paintings were taken from the Bible, mythology, and history. He realistically depicted the persons and events of his own time, as for example, the Americans in his unfinished painting of the revolutionary peace negotiations (*see* p. 257). Although he supported America during the Revolution, he avoided painting any scenes of British defeats, leaving these to Trumbull because he did not want to lose the king's support. He died in England on March 11, 1820.

WHEATLEY, Phillis (1753?–1784). America's first black poet was born in Africa and brought to Boston aboard a slave ship about 1761. She was purchased by a prosperous tailor, John Wheatley, as a maid for his wife. As was the custom, Phillis took her last name from

Phillis Wheatley

her owner. The Wheatleys taught Phillis how to read and write, and about the age of 13, she began composing poetry. In 1773, Wheatley's son Nathaniel took Phillis to England for her health, and there her first volume of poems was published. The trip was cut short by news that Mrs. Wheatley was dying. Phillis was freed after Mrs. Wheatley's death and became a supporter of the Revolution. She praised George Washington in a poem that included the phrase, *"Thee, first in peace and honours."* The general was so flattered that he granted her a personal interview. Phillis died a pauper in Boston in 1784 and was buried in an unmarked grave.

WILKINSON, James (1757–1825). A man who spent his life involved in intrigues for power and money, Wilkinson is believed responsible for divulging the plot of **Thomas Conway** (*see*) and others to have George Washington removed from command of the Continental Army in 1777. Wilkinson had served under **Benedict Arnold** (*see*) at Quebec in 1776 and was an aide to **Horatio Gates** (*see*) in the Saratoga campaign of 1777. Congress reprimanded him for his slowness in bringing the news of that victory. Nevertheless, Congress commissioned him a brigadier general. Wilkinson was appointed secretary to the Board of War in 1778, but he was forced to resign the post because of his apparent involvement in the plot to replace Washington with Gates. He became clothier general of the army in 1779 but was forced to resign in 1781 because of irregularities in his accounts. Wilkinson moved to the Kentucky region in 1784 and engaged in trading ventures and land speculations. He returned to the army in 1791 and served under **Anthony Wayne** (*see*), whom he secretly tried to discredit. Wilkinson was made governor of the Louisiana Territory in 1805 but was removed from office the following year because of his unpopularity. During his governorship, he was implicated with Aaron Burr (1756–1836) in an attempt to establish trading monopolies in the territory. Wilkinson was investigated several times by Congress. He was court-martialed in 1811 but found innocent of irregularities in his dealings with the Spanish. During the War of 1812, he was relieved of command after an unsuccessful expedition against Montreal. Wilkinson died in Mexico in 1825 while seeking a land grant in present-day Texas.

WILSON, James (1742–1798). Wilson, a Scottish-born lawyer, was one of the first colonists to conclude that Parliament had no authority over the American colonies. In 1774, he wrote that he could find no "constitutional line" acknowledging Parliament's power. Later, as a member of the committee that wrote the United States Constitution in 1787, Wilson advocated that the President and members of both houses of Congress be elected by popular vote. Wilson was a member of the Second Continental Congress (*see* **Continental Congress**) in 1776 and was at first a proponent of a strong national government. His defense of British loyalists as well as land speculations and trade interests led to an attack on his home by the Philadelphia militia in 1779. A few persons were killed before Wilson was rescued. In 1782, Wilson was elected to the Congress of the Confederation and also served in it from 1785 to 1787. He was appointed an Associate Justice of the United States Supreme Court in 1789.

WITHERSPOON, John (1723–1794). Witherspoon, a Presbyterian minister who was a signer of the **Declaration of Independence** (*see*), was a major influence in American religion, education, and politics at the time of the Revolution. He was born in Scotland and received a divinity degree from the University of Edinburgh in 1743. He preached in the town of Paisley until 1768, when he immigrated to America to become president of the College of New Jersey (now Princeton University), a position he held until his death. Witherspoon, whose philosophy was "common sense," enlarged the school's curriculum to include courses designed to train men for civic leadership. Among his students who later rose to national prominence was James Madison (1751–1836), the fourth President of the United States. In 1774, Witherspoon joined the movement for independence, urging colonists "to declare the firm resolve never to submit to the claims of Great Britain, but deliberately to prefer war with all its horrors, and even extermination to slavery." In 1776, Witherspoon took part in the ouster of the royalist governor of New Jersey, William Franklin (1731–1813). As a delegate to the Second Continental Congress, Witherspoon urged the adoption of the Declaration. During his Congressional service, he was a member of more than 100 committees. After the war, Witherspoon devoted himself to rebuilding his college.

Witherspoon resided in the president's mansion opposite Nassau Hall.